THE LUNCH LADIES

CULTIVATING AN ACTSMOSPHERE

PHILIP JENKINS

© 2015 Philip Jenkins

All rights reserved. No part of the publication may be reproduced, stored in a retrieval system, or transmitted in any form of by any means without the prior written permission of the author. The only exception is brief quotations in printed reviews.

ISBN-13: 978-1505509939

Printed by Creative Graphics
100 Oak St. Lebanon, TN 37087
www.creativegraphics.net

Unless otherwise indicated, all Scripture quotations are from The Holy Bible, English Standard Version®, copyright © 2001 by Crossway, a publishing ministry of Good News Publishers. Used by permission. All rights reserved.

NEW INTERNATIONAL VERSION®. Copyright © 1973, 1978, 1984 by Biblica, Inc. All rights reserved worldwide. Used by permission.
NEW INTERNATIONAL VERSION® and NIV® are registered trademarks of Biblica, Inc. Use of either trademark for the offering of goods or services requires the prior written consent of Biblica US, Inc.

Scripture taken from the New King James Version®. Copyright © 1982 by Thomas Nelson. Used by permission. All rights reserved.

CONTENTS

	What People Are Saying about *The Lunch Ladies*	7
	Foreword by David Shannon	11
	Preface	13
	Acknowledgements	15
	Glossary of Terms	17

PART 1

1	Between the Bells	21
2	The Cafeteria	25
3	The Day Indifference Died	29
4	Esmin Green	33
5	Aftermath	43
6	We Feel Awkward so You Don't Have To	49
7	Discovering Electricity	57

PART 2

8	Life and Godliness	65
9	The Lunch Lady I Never Met	71
10	The Courage for Faith	79
11	The Power of an Invitation	85
12	More Than You Think	95
13	In Their Own Words	101

PART 3

14	Preparing the Soil	109
15	Recruiting	115
16	Meeting Expectations	131
17	Failure to Lunch	151
18	The Book Is Ending. The Story Is Not.	161

	Appendix I: F.A.Q.s	171
	Appendix II: Preparing for Launch	181
	Appendix III: The Lunch Ladies Covenant	182

WHAT PEOPLE ARE SAYING ABOUT
THE LUNCH LADIES

"We take our Fundamentals of Youth and Family Ministry class at Freed-Hardeman University on a field trip to the Mt. Juliet church of Christ each semester to look at, listen to, and learn from Philip Jenkins and David Shannon. It was during one of those visits that Philip told us about the Lunch Ladies program. I was excited about the program when I heard about it and I am proud that he is putting this book into print. It addresses something that I emphasize regularly when doing personal evangelism workshops. This book will become one of the required texts in our Youth and Family Ministry program at F.H.U."

- Kirk Brothers, Assistant Professor,
Freed-Hardeman University

. . . .

Spiritual Outward Bound. That's how I describe some of the short-term mission trips I've heard about. Outward Bound is a wilderness program that teaches self-esteem, survival, self-examination, and self-confrontation. People learn to navigate in the woods but no one ever gets lost. People learn to rock climb but no one ever takes a lead fall. People learn to live off the land but no one ever starves. It's a contrived experience. It's very powerful. It's very transforming but it's not the same as real life or death survival. Mission trips involve going, seeing, and doing. They are often moving, transformational, and beneficial. But in the end the focus seems to be a bit self-serving. I'm not saying that they are bad or ineffective. But what I have observed is that participants talk about what they saw and felt, and how they changed. I always thought missions were about changing other people.

The originator of the phrase "Significant Obscurity" properly defined what servant evangelism is about. We don't have to be well known, famous, or nationwide. We just have to be significant to the people we influence. Opportunity equals responsibility. Mark Sanborn describes it as giving people in our immediate area of influence attention, belonging, and support. Tim Frizzell describes it as seeing needs, making connections, promoting relationships, preparing for transitions, and intervening in crisis. The apostle Paul describes it as the members having the same care one for another (1 Corinthians 12:25).

Philip Jenkins has taken all those things--things based solidly in the Word of God, things that epitomize the idea that the church is not an organization but rather an organism--and has summed it up in a way that only he can. I've never used the word Fwednesday (that's the first time I've ever written it!). I don't use words like Actsmosphere or successipes...I use words like S.W.A.T. and tactics, shepherd warrior, spiritual self-reliance....and I use them because I like the way they make me feel about me and how they describe me. Philip Jenkins has a ministry called Lunch Ladies. **Nothing** in the term, concept, definition, or execution has anything to do about self--other than each self conforming to the servant leadership, compassion, and mission of Jesus. Lunch Ladies is not about transforming **us**. It is about seeking, loving, serving, and transforming **others**. In order to do that, we must be that. When that change comes from a focus on others rather than self, then we understand what it is to **be** a Lunch Lady, an evangelist, a servant, a Christlike person.

Peter wanted to die defending Jesus. He wanted to earn his martyr badge. (If God wanted a soldier, He could have raised David or sent Michael the archangel). But when He wanted to define Peter, He simply said, "Do you love Me? Feed My lambs."

Lunch Ladies and lamb feeding. Pretty awesome.

To God be the glory.

Thank you, Philip.

-Lonnie Jones
Licensed Professional Counselor

. . . .

A couple of years ago when I first heard David Shannon and then later Philip Jenkins talk about the concept of "Lunch Ladies," I was immediately intrigued. When they described the way their youth group used to be, it was exactly the frustration that I was feeling with my youth group. I could also tell you exactly which teens would sit together, which teens would talk to other teens, and the worst part-- which teens were no longer coming to youth events or worship services at all because of the way they were being treated or ignored.

I tried several things and had definitely taught that "you shouldn't treat others badly," but nothing had worked so far. I was at a level of hopelessness and despair.

Over the next few months, I spent a great deal of time studying and learning about the Lunch Ladies concept; we implemented it here about seven months ago after our Spring Retreat. It has been the largest contributing factor in a complete cultural change.

Within the first two months, I had many parents and teens come up to me and say, "I am so excited about what you are doing to stop the issues we have with cliques. I can already tell things are so much better." I had kids that had given up on the youth group tell me that with the exception of a couple of kids, everyone now loves everyone and that is a huge change from just a few weeks ago.

Within the first few months, we had several baptisms that I contribute in large part to the outreach of this program. The teens in the Lunch Ladies began to reach out to other teens, and those began to attend services. They began to see the love of Jesus lived out, and it has truly changed them.

The following are quotes from two of our teens that are participants in the Lunch Ladies program.

> "Lunch Ladies has impacted our youth group by helping connect the youth all around. We've seen an enormous amount of improvement and we've seen the 'cliques' slowly decreasing.

It has helped bring our group closer and it will help visitors in the future feel welcome."

"Lunch Ladies for us has been a really great experience. I believe it has brought the members in the group a whole lot closer and created better and more powerful connections. I know it has brought many visitors and some new members to our church. I have created many more friendships and am so glad for it!"

If you are experiencing any problems with unity in your youth group or if you want to stretch and grow beyond what you can imagine, begin the Lunch Ladies program today in your youth group. You will not be sorry you did!

- Joey Markham
Youth Minister, Germantown church of Christ

FOREWORD

When you hear the term *Lunch Lady*, what comes to mind?

Hair nets?

Mystery meat and green peas?

Not anymore!

It's surprising just how much that term has come to mean to us at the Mt. Juliet church of Christ.

The process is Biblical while the creative flair is Philip Jenkins. I've stopped being surprised by his off-the-charts creativity, but I am continually impressed by what breaks his heart. Thankfully Philip's heart, like many of yours, has been broken by youth, and adults for that matter, who are satisfied with the country club culture of some churches or youth groups.

And I'm equally impressed by his willingness to always search for godly solutions. After prayer and study, he stepped into a classroom and challenged youth to examine their beliefs about their purpose as a group. In your hands you hold a written description of an amazing godly solution to transforming apathetic cultures into vibrant, living reflections of Christ.

Should the church be a place the sick come to be ignored?

Pause and reread that.

Lives were powerfully transformed in the months that followed. The word *transformed* isn't used lightly here. I guess I never thought I would see the day when teens would not only invite others to class but also go to class intending for no person to sit alone. I started hearing about situations like a visitor walking in late and sitting down by himself only to have one of our youth get up out of his chair to go sit next to the guest. I heard about our youth making sure everyone was talked with--not just spoken to, but brought into conversations and activities. I wanted to cheer!

Major transformation was happening not only in the lives of our youth but also in the lives of the many guests who were being shown the love of Christ! Remember, the greatest commandment is love. Our teens were doing their best to live Christ's love, and just as you might expect, love is loud--you can't ignore it, and you've got to love it! It made guests genuinely want to come back. Over the next few months, more and more returned. This gave opportunities for further studies. The truth of God continued to transform their lives as the waters of baptism were frequently stirring.

So many of our teens have left their comfort zones, moved by the godly principles that guide the "Lunch Ladies." The concept isn't new: loving others (Matthew 22:37), having genuine interest in their interests (Philippians 2:4), but especially in their souls (Matthew 28:19-20).

The culture of the Mt. Juliet youth group has changed, the youth have changed, many have been saved, and the mushroom effect is that our adults are adopting a similar model and other youth groups have started their versions, too. The population of Heaven is already greater!

I pray this book will help you and your ministry on your road to transformation as well. It isn't about Philip, or Mt. Juliet, but about God's Kingdom.

Glory to the King of Kings for saving sinners like me.

- David Shannon
Minister, Mt. Juliet church of Christ

PREFACE

I have to confess that it's always been a dream of mine to write a book, but what I didn't want was to write a book just for the sake of saying "Hey, look! I wrote a book!" (and other rhyming things).

The other thing that has kept me from writing is I didn't want to write a book that has already been written. There have been thousands of books written about ministry, Christianity, and youth ministry--books written by experts and books that I've been blessed by--well, at least the two that I've read.

I'm grateful that those two obstacles have been removed: this is the book I wanted to write.

This book is not about me. In fact, the only reason I'm in it is because God has been so gracious to give me a seat on His roller coaster. I'm not the one who designed or invented the roller coaster--I'm just getting to watch it from up close.

I firmly believe this book is going to help people. I don't know of another book out there quite like it, but then again, there are a lot of books out there, so odds are there might be one. I just haven't seen it yet. And that's why I'm writing this. I believe this book can--no, I believe **God can**--use this book to bless hundreds of thousands of lives.

I pray, and I truly mean this, that this book will serve as a powerful tool in helping Christians relentlessly pursue souls.

The book is divided into three major sections:

> PART 1 entitled "The Cafeteria" will give you a glimpse into the culture of indifference that had become the norm for our group. Perhaps you will see some familiar characteristics in your congregation or youth program.

In PART 2 called "Successipes," I will share with you a few amazing stories that have served as a testimony of God's power at work through the Lunch Ladies ministry. I pray there are many more.

And finally PART 3, "Your Cafeteria," will serve as a practical how-to guide in helping you cast, kickstart, and cultivate a contagious kind of ministry where you live.

I cannot wait to share this story, this ministry, this book, this blessing with you! May God bless you with many more "successipes" of His love and His power!

ACKNOWLEDGEMENTS

This book would not have happened if not for the following individuals. I owe each of them in a way that I could never repay.

Laura, my wife, my best friend, thank you for keeping Christ before me. In a very real way, you are the reason this book exists. The Lunch Ladies ministry and its people are close to my heart because of the way you first showed Christ's love to me at a time when I needed it most. I knew that you were special then, and I've never forgotten it. I love you.

Mom and Dad, thank you for showing me what a Christian home looks like.

Andrew, thank you for liking my ideas enough to encourage me to continue dreaming.

To David Shannon, you make everyone a little better. Thank you for your friendship, your wisdom, and your encouragement.

To Tonja McRady, thank you not only for your fantastic, editorial, proofreading eye, but for the way that you believed in this book throughout the process. Your heart shined through in every suggestion and critique.

Scott Utter, thank you for once again nailing the artwork and for formatting this book. You are enormously talented, my friend.

To the Lunch Ladies, thank you for making ministry fun. This is the most amazing, exciting, rewarding thing I have ever been a part of in youth ministry. You have taught me much.

Finally, this book would not be possible if not for Mark DeVries. Mark, thank you for writing *Sustainable Youth Ministry*, and thank you especially for the things you shared in your chapter entitled "The Magnet Effect."

And above all, thank you "...to Him who is able to do immeasurably more than all we ask or imagine, according to His power that is at work within us, to Him be glory in the church and in Christ Jesus throughout all generations, for ever and ever! Amen" (Ephesians 3:20-21, NIV).

GLOSSARY OF TERMS

ACTMOSPHERE: having the characteristics of the church's atmosphere in the book of Acts--loving, selfless, sacrificial, united, devoted, fellowship-filled, believing, awe-filled, together, need-meeting, glad, generous, praising, favorable, evangelistic, and growing.

ALL FOR ONE: the name given to the adult version of the Lunch Ladies ministry that we do on a congregational level at Mt. Juliet. Every Sunday morning adult Bible class has an All For One group. Most of them meet every two weeks and zero in on reaching people that are in their demographic. Because our congregation has a shepherding model in place, every Sunday morning adult Bible class also has an elder in it who is closely connected to the people inside of that room. In addition, every Sunday morning adult Bible class has a class coordinator who is in charge of "running the meeting" effectively. It is important for this person to have a good grasp of what the purpose of the All For One ministry is.

COCOON LEADERS: 28 adults that have made a commitment to work with our students for an entire school year on Wednesday nights. There are 2 Cocoon Leaders per Cocoon (2 per gender per grade), and they generally move up with the students as the students get older.

COCOONS: The name we gave to our small group ministry at Mt. Juliet. The word is symbolic in that cocoons represent a place to weather storms, small spaces where great transformations take place, a place for those who struggle, a place to find new life in Christ, a place to grow, a place to become something even more beautiful, a place of preparation, a temporary home, a place of protection, a place of refuge, a work in progress, the concept of "out with the old, in with the new," a place where we learn to fly.

FWEDNESDAY: Friend + Wednesday = *Fwednesday!* These are special Wednesday nights that we hold about once a quarter where we encourage all of our students to bring a friend. We meet early, play games, eat some food, connect with some new people, and have a guest speaker.

<u>LUNCH LADIES</u>: the nickname given to a group of our students who made it their mission to put an end to a culture of neglect within our youth program. Lunch Ladies are the only people in the cafeteria who make sure that everybody is served.

<u>SUCCESSIPES</u>: a success story that brings honor to God.

<u>TAKE ROUTE</u>: a Bible study that I wrote and use in one-on-one settings to lead people to the Lord. Many are using these books in their ministries, and it's even available in Spanish. If you'd like to order some, email me at <u>philmycup@hotmail.com</u>!

PART 1
THE CAFETERIA

1

BETWEEN THE BELLS

THE SUBJECT WE ALL MUST STUDY

I spent the better part of the 7th grade (even though there is no such thing as a better part of the 7th grade) bitter, lonely, and desperate to fit in. I'd say that I didn't have a friend in the world at that point, except that that's not entirely true: my best friend in the 7th grade was my English teacher Mrs. Hoskins.

My dad decided to ruin my life by moving our family from the small town of Hamilton, Alabama, into Nashville, Tennessee. I know, right? What tyranny!

I was devastated. I was alone. I was hurting.

I was the new kid.

I remember going the entire school day without anyone talking to me. I dressed funny, I talked funny, I looked funny, and in 7th grade--let's be real--I smelled funny.

I was homesick.

Here's the thing about moving: it's not just moving to a new place that's tough--it's leaving your life behind in the place that you move from.

"At least Opryland will be there," I thought. It permanently closed right before we moved.

"At least I'll have basketball," I thought. I hated the basketball program at the new school so much that I quit the following summer, which also put a damper on my life-long dream of playing in the NBA.

"At least my dad promised to take me to see Michael Jordan play if we move," I thought. He retired...for the second (or third? or fourth?) time.

What was going on? It was almost as if God hadn't been following the script I had written for my life.

I wish I could say that I was reading my Bible when a deep spiritual truth hit me between the eyes, or at the very least that an angel appeared to me riding a Harley with a flaming sword in his teeth and an American flag in his hand to give me some sort of revelation...although I'm pretty sure I just described Ghost Rider.

You see, life isn't like school, where the lessons are presented within windows of time, periods of learning timed by bells. In school the teacher says, "Ok, class, today we're going to learn about the difference in stalactites and stalagmites, so everybody get your pencils and textbooks out...the ones with all of the answers filled in."

Life isn't like that at all.

Here in the real world, you can't really anticipate when life's most important lessons are going to be taught. The most important lessons in life aren't learned in 50 minutes between the sounding of two bells. Here in reality, it's more like our homeroom teacher went rogue and threw out the curriculum, textbooks, and lesson plans and ignored all of the bells.

Seemingly, there are some courses in life that are offered strictly on sleepless nights. Nights that could be characterized by words like *heart-wrenching, tearful, long, painful, heartbreaking, frustrating, lonely, angry, desperate, hopeful,* and *hopeless.* It seems the only way to learn those types of lessons is to log a lot of those types of days and nights, and hope that eventually the clouds will unfurl and the light will come on.

You'll look back on the places that you've visited along the way. You'll remember the pain, but you'll also go, "Hey, look at this cool souvenir I picked up while I was stranded at that rest stop on I-65," or "You see that dent in my car? Let me tell you what I learned about bears that day." Sometimes life feels like you're going sightseeing, except nobody told you exactly what you were supposed to be seeing. Our hope needs to be that by the time we leave, we figure out what those things were.

It has taken me a lot of years to see it, but I believe God was teaching me something about loneliness in the 7th grade.

Loneliness is not a 7th grade subject; loneliness goes to kindergarten, middle school, high school, and beyond. It goes to the cafeteria. It goes to P.E., and then it takes the bus at the end of the day. It goes to work. It goes to church. It goes home. It hangs out with you in your room. It drives a car. It listens to music. It reads books. It comes to dinner. It goes to bed. It sits alone with you in the dark. It cries. You set your alarm, and so does loneliness.

No, loneliness is not a 7th grade subject--it is a subject we all must study.

. . . .

FRIENDSHIP OR BUSSED

I don't remember the first time I met her. I probably said something like "Hi, my name is Philip," in the thickest, most Alabama-accent there is. And she probably said something eloquent like, "Hi. I'm Laura. It's nice to meet you." (She always did know just what to say.)

But one of my earliest memories of Laura Manning came on the 8th grade trip to Washington, D.C. / New York. It had been a long day of sightseeing in Washington. It was a late night and as you can imagine on a bus full of 8th graders, there was an unfamiliar, welcome sound: quiet. But as the bus quietly rolled along that night, the familiar feelings of my heart once again echoed loudly in my mind: "Nobody likes you.

Nobody cares. You don't fit in here. You're an idiot. You're a loser. You don't have any friends. You're alone. And you'll always be that way."

Laura turned around in her seat. "Hey, so how are you doing?"

It's crazy and it probably sounds cheesy, but Laura choosing to turn around and ask me that question was the beginning of a friendship that turned my life around.

This 8th grade girl, this person who cared enough about me to ask how I was doing, this Christian (in the truest sense of the word) taught me something that day that still rings as true to me in 2015 as it did to me back then.

It may sound simple, but it doesn't make it any less true. I have discovered that there is at least one thing that everybody in this world needs, no matter how young or how old you are: a friend. Someone who genuinely cares about you, someone who shows you that you matter by investing his life, his time, his heart, his concern into you.

People matter. Souls matter. And all people, all souls have hurt. If we will only stop to pay attention, lives will be changed forever.

2

THE CAFETERIA

HIDE AND GO SEAT

I want to close your eyes and reimagine one of the most horrifyingly brutal places on planet Earth. A place so vile that unless it's a part of your world (I'm singing "The Little Mermaid") right now, you've probably blocked it out and removed it far from your memory. A place you left behind and never looked back (unless your name is Uncle Rico).

High school...I almost threw the word *musical* in there, and I guess that would've fit the bill, too. But seriously, I'm not sure you could convince any adult in his right mind to go back through those four (hopefully) years.

There's a reason that people make jokes about "that guy" that never "leaves" high school. It's because it's messed up to want to go back there and live. I've started thinking about it this way: if a guy's longing to go back to high school, his life must really be that bad. Let's face it: high school is hard.

Now I want you to picture your high school cafeteria.

Ah, lunchtime. Your favorite subject.

You push through the doors and take a deep breath. You smell that? Smells like teen spirit and sloppy joes, my friend.

You haven't thought about this place in years, yet you're surprised at how familiar it is to you. The memories come flooding back. The textbooks out on the table. The last-minute cramming for the test next period that you've already heard is impossible no matter how much you study. The overachiever doing the math homework that had only been assigned ten minutes ago.

The noise. You forgot what the sound of 300 teenagers eating at once sounded like.

Wait, was it always this loud? And how in the world could they possibly be focusing on doing their math homework--oh, they're copying each other's homework. Well, that makes sense.

And just as you are about to ask Jennifer to wear your jersey on game day, your game gets interrupted.

"CRASH! CLING, cling, cling, cling, cling, cling! WRRRRR, wrrr, wrr, wrr, wrrrrrrrrrrrrrr!!!" The sound fills the entire room like a crashing cymbal, and all eyes turn toward the new girl.

You know the new girl, right? Oh wait, no you don't, but you do now: the new girl that dropped her lunch tray in the cafeteria on her first day.

There's a three-second delay, followed by some cheers and applause-- not exactly the way she was looking to begin her high school career. Luckily for her, only 13 of the generous 20 minutes assigned for lunch remain.

The pace is hurried. You glance over and see the long line of people waiting to pay for their food--Reason #27 why you bring your own lunch. (Yes, you actually have a list. No, nobody actually knows that.)

And as you open up that crinkly, brown paper bag you're reminded of Reason #28 why you bring your own lunch: Hot Pockets. You love Hot Pockets...not that you'd actually admit to that either. Besides, if people knew how much you loved Hot Pockets they wouldn't let you sit--

And that's when it dawns on you that you have an important decision to make: where are you going to sit?

Your eyes scan the room.

To your immediate right is a table full of girls. "Hey, that could be fun," you think to yourself, but quickly talk yourself out of it after remembering that you went with the meatball Hot Pocket.

You check the room again.

A table full of baseball guys is towards the back. Then there's the table where the band sits, the cheerleaders' table, the Book Club (they don't call themselves that, but you do), the misfits, the football team, the guys who like to play *Magic: The Gathering*, the popular kids, the guys who like to talk about mudding and camo and blowing stuff up.

So, where are you going to sit?

3

THE DAY INDIFFERENCE DIED

....

DOWN WITH THE SICKNESS

Youth ministry is the greatest job in the world, but there were some things about it that were beginning to make me sick.

Looking back, things weren't going poorly. Actually things were going pretty well. My wife and I had been working with the youth at Mt. Juliet church of Christ for about a year and half. We loved the church (and still do!). We had great involvement, an active, event-rich youth program, and buy-in from almost everybody--the eldership, the students, and the parents.

Still, something wasn't right; I just couldn't quite put my finger on it...

....

DECISION TIME

It was Wednesday, February 22, 2012. I remember it just like it was today (I have a hard time remembering yesterday).

On Wednesday nights I taught the high school class. Each week anywhere between 45-60 kids crammed into a narrow room in a downstairs area of the church building that people had affectionately nicknamed "The Youth Dungeon." It lived up to its name, too--it was so creepy.

I remember being excited. Excited because I had one of those classes: a class I felt good about. Those don't come along as frequently as we ministers would like, so we sort of get excited about them.

I had a good feeling about this night. We were studying through the book of Acts, and on this particular evening we were getting ready to tackle Acts 6, a story about widows being neglected.

I admit it sounds pretty weird (and a little bit twisted) for me to be excited about talking to high school students about widows being neglected, but here's why I was excited: teenagers connect with idea of neglect. And while most teens can't identify with the idea of being a widow, they can identify with the idea of being neglected.

6:45 p.m. Showtime.

I walked downstairs and began making my way through the narrow corridor of the youth dungeon and finally into the youth room.

The sight stopped me in my tracks.

"Where is everybody?"

Did I say that out loud?

"Oh, there's an El Salvador mission team meeting tonight."

Apparently I did.

"You've got to be kidding me," I thought to myself, making sure it wasn't out loud.

The students in my class weren't "spiritual kids." All of the "spiritual kids" were getting ready to go to El Salvador to do mission work.

And I almost feel ashamed for the next thought that passed through my mind (and some of you readers will identify with this): "Should I 'waste' this class? Shouldn't I save it until the whole group could hear it?

Maybe I could do something else off the top of my head (every minister has a "go-to" lesson for occasions such as this--I'm looking at you, "Five-Finger Prayer").

These thoughts swirled around inside my head as I semi-enthusiastically shook hands with a couple of first-time guests named Chris and Alex.

The room was 70% empty, or 30% full if you're crazy optimistic.

But now it was 7:00. Time for class to begin. Time to make a decision...

4

ESMIN GREEN

....

WHAT I SAID

The following is my manuscript from class that night:

"Have you guys heard about Jeremy Lin and the Linsanity that has been taking place over the last few weeks? It's been Lincredible. The guy has been playing out of his mind and has led the Knicks to victory after victory these last several days. It's been awesome to watch.

However, this past week the Knicks lost their first game in nearly two weeks. But that's not the big story. The big story is someone over at ESPN decided after the game to run this unfortunate headline: "Chink in the Armor," which is offensive to people of Asian descent.

What was the motive behind the headline? Nobody can be sure, but one thing's for sure: the employee responsible for the headline got fired.[1]

You see, sometimes the motive really isn't all that important. What matters are the facts.

Tonight, a story in Acts 6 that honestly I have questions about. I don't understand the motives behind it.

---

[1] http://www.forbes.com/sites/gregorymcneal/2012/02/18/espn-uses-chink-in-the-armor-line- twice-did-linsanity-just-go-racist/

Acts 6:1 says, "Now in these days when the disciples were increasing in number, a complaint by the Hellenists arose against the Hebrews because their widows were being neglected in the daily distribution."

Good news: disciples were increasing in number. Bad news: some widows were being overlooked. They depended on that daily distribution of food. Their husbands couldn't provide for them anymore and so they needed assistance. So here we probably have at least some sweet older ladies who weren't able to get food.

I'd like to say that it was just a simple mistake. You know, just an oversight.

But there's more bad news: this wasn't a one-time thing. It kept happening to a certain group of widows--Hellenists, the Greek-speaking Jews that had become Christians. In other words, widows who spoke a different language. They didn't speak Hebrew.

And so here were these widows who spoke another language and weren't getting food that they needed. It'd be like us having a food pantry here at church for our widows but not including any widows from our Hispanic brothers and sisters.

What do you think? Do you think this happened by accident or was this done on purpose?

The motive isn't really the point. The point is people who are in need are being neglected. That's a problem. And in the church, if it isn't dealt with quickly and in the right way, then it becomes a real problem.

The next six verses talk about how the Apostles wisely handled the situation with the widows. They selected a few good men who handled the responsibility of making sure none of them were overlooked.

I want to show you guys a powerful clip.[2] (I recommend stopping here and watching it before reading any further.)

"A sad death in New York City. Surveillance cameras in a city-run psychiatric hospital emergency room in Brooklyn capture a woman falling from a chair, writhing on the floor, and dying. Hospital staff and other patients watch and do nothing for over an hour. One guard doesn't even leave his chair, rolling it around the corner to stare at the body. The New York Civil Liberties Union sued the facility, King's County Hospital Center, last year over the way it treats psychiatric patients. The city's medical examiner has yet to determine why the woman, 49-year-old Esmin Green, died on June 20. She had been waiting in the emergency room for nearly 24 hours.

"'The reason this woman died the way she did is because there is a culture of indifference to patients that permeates every aspect of K.C.H.C.'s psychiatric care' —Rob Cohen (attorney).

"The agency that runs the hospital released a statement saying, 'We are shocked and distressed by the situation. It is clear that some of our employees failed to act based on our compassionate standards of care. (The hospital has) directed the suspension and termination of those involved.'"

"Surveillance video eventually shows a member of the medical staff attending to Green, but it is too late: she has already died."—End transcript

Who was Esmin Green? Esmin Green was a 49-year-old woman who died in the very place where she was supposed to get help. That's what a hospital does, right? It's a place that helps people.

The lawyer from the video talked about how they were seeking to put an end to a culture of neglect.

---

[2] https://www.youtube.com/watch?v=9IKUwBCIBzA

That story gives me chills...and it disturbs me, because I fear that Esmin Green walks through the doors of our church building and comes into our youth group week after week.

Guys, I've got to be honest. This might be harsh, but I feel like I need to say this to you: There is a culture of neglect in this youth group.

What I'm saying is, I come in here week after week, and I know exactly where you're going to sit, and whom you will talk to and whom you won't. I know who will sit by themselves.

I fear that we have a culture of neglect within our youth group.

What if that became our youth group motto? "We seek an end to the culture of neglect."

In the 7th grade I moved to Nashville. I didn't know a single person at my school. I remember entire days where I could go without a single person talking to me. You want to know a lonely feeling? Feeling neglected. Feeling invisible.

Now going back to Acts: What was the reason behind the widows being neglected?

Was it because the church was growing so quickly and getting so large that they didn't know these widows? Was it because they didn't like Hellenists? Was it because those widows spoke a different language? Was it simply because they didn't know them as well?

What was the reason for neglect?

You want to know the reason for neglect? **The reason doesn't matter**--because **people** were being neglected.

What's your reason for not talking to that person inside this room that's a little different?

"Oh, that person's a snob!"

"Oh, that person is weird."

"Oh, it's really awkward talking to people I don't know very well."

"Um, I don't know that person's name and I should."

"Oh, I didn't neglect them--I spoke to them! I mean, that visitor was in my seat, so I asked them to move because I had it reserved for someone else."

Listen, the reason for the neglect that happens in our youth group isn't important. The reason doesn't matter--because **people** are being neglected.

What's important is that an Esmin Green comes in here, hurting and in need, but so many don't even notice or pretend to care.

I really want to make a point here, but what I'm about to share with you cannot leave this room. [Note: I changed these names so that the people's identities would remain anonymous.]

This information in the wrong hands could hurt someone else's feelings, and that's not the point. The point isn't to point at others. The point is pointed at us, not these people. So I need you to be mature with what I'm about to share with you. How many of you can do that?

I'm going to put six names on the screen.

Aarek Johnson, Tyler Valentine, Brett Holmes, Jennifer Pate, Mary Thomas, Jud Holloway.

I want you to be honest: First of all, I want to ask you how many of you know at least one of the people on that list? Raise your hands.

How many of you know two? (I looked around the room. A few hands went up.)

Three? (A lot of hands went down.)

Four? (A lot more hands went down.)

Five?

All six? (By this time no hands were left.)

Did you know that two of the six were baptized in the last year? Did you know that out of the six, four of them are in high school? Did you know that four out of these six people haven't been to church on a Wednesday night maybe ever? Did you know that one of these six has just started coming? Did you know that one out of these six sits inside of this classroom every week?

Now, I didn't put this one on the screen, but if I were to say the name Katerina Rogers, would it mean anything to you?

Guys, she's been here every week for probably the past 20 weeks straight, but how many of you have taken the time to even learn her name, speak to her, or tell her your name?

Who is your Esmin Green, and what are you going to do about it? Remember the security guard from the video? He came into the room, looked at her, and didn't so much as get out of his seat to check on her. Are you like that? Do you really care for the people that come inside this room?

Matthew 25:42-46 says, "'For I was hungry and you gave Me no food, I was thirsty and you gave Me no drink, I was a stranger and you did not welcome Me, naked and you did not clothe Me, sick and in prison and you did not visit Me.' Then they also will answer, saying, 'Lord, when did we see You hungry or thirsty or a stranger or naked or sick or in prison, and did not minister to You?' Then He will answer them, saying, 'Truly, I say to you, as you did not do it to one of the least of these, you did not do it to Me.' And these will go away into eternal punishment, but the righteous into eternal life."

"Jesus, when did we see **You** sick? Because, Lord, if **You** were sick, we would've definitely helped **You**! I mean, are You sure we saw **You**? I don't remember seeing **You**, Lord. Where were **You**?"

Jesus says, "I was Esmin Green! You don't remember Me, because you neglected Me. I was the least of these, that person that you thought of least. I was sick and you didn't take care of Me. I was sitting in the room and you ignored Me. I was hurting and you turned a blind eye towards Me."

This is another one of those things that I'm not sure I should tell you...

I got a text the other day from a girl in our youth group who said, "I'm going to start visiting other churches."

I said, "Oh, man. I hate to hear that! Why? What's up? Is there anything I can do?"

She said, "I have no friends and I get left out on a lot of things. I just don't really feel welcomed. That's why I don't come to class."

I basically begged. "Hey, I'm your friend. Hang in there. Is there anything I can do?

And then I said, "What if we both pray about this? And we ask God to send you a friend? Would you give God a chance to answer that prayer?" She said, "Yes."

A part of me wants to tell you who it is. But how about this? Instead of me telling you who said it, I think I'd rather let you wonder about every single possibility, every single name, that's running through your mind right now.

Guys, I long for the day when you guys take it upon yourselves to make sure that every single person who comes into this room is treated like he or she really matters to you. I long for the day when every single person who comes into this room is treated like Jesus.

I'm tired of seeing neglect. I hate neglect. I hate the similarities that I see between this room and a high school lunchroom, where every clique has a section. Hey, if you can't get help inside of the church-- God's hospital--where in the world can you get it?

I can tell you one thing: If someone chooses not to come back here, I don't ever want to hear that it's because nobody cared.

I don't talk straight with you guys very often. But when I look at our youth group, I'm not proud of the little groups that ignore each other. Oh, we can pretend that they're not there, but it's naive. Guys, this weekend's trip would be a great time to turn a corner.

Here's how we're going to wrap up tonight. I want you to take that little note card, turn it over, and write down these two questions:

1. Who is someone that has come here before needing to be reached?
2. What will I do to reach them tonight?

If you need some help answering that one, let me know tonight. I've got a whole youth directory of kids that need reaching.

Who is someone in this room tonight that I need to check on? Who is someone in this room that your heart feels the need to speak to or reach out to?

Tonight we're going to end class a little differently. In just a minute, I want you to do something. I want you to find someone in this room that you don't usually talk to. And we're going to take the rest of the time to do this.

I want you to get with that person and spend some time checking in with them spiritually. So I want you to partner up, and spread out. Find a place to go and pray together. And then we're just going to ask each other a simple question: How are you doing spiritually?

Let's designate this room as a room where the girls can pray together, so that they can have some privacy. But take as much time as you need.

Let's bow and have a prayer, and then I'll let you guys disperse."

Note: I want to be fair to Esmin Green's story. This is a story about a patient with a mental illness being ignored in the waiting room of a mental hospital. On one hand, this book does not specifically speak to the way that we as the church ought to treat those who are suffering from mental illness. On the other hand, it does: we are to treat everyone like Jesus, regardless of a person's mental, physical, or spiritual health. May we all be moved with the compassion of our Savior.

5

AFTERMATH

CRYING OUT

After I dismissed the groups for prayer, one of the girls in the class made her way to the front to approach me.

"Hey, Juliebeth. What's up?" I smiled.

"Philip," she began as tears began to roll down her face. "You have to share that with the rest of the group this weekend."

"You think so?"

"Yes. It's something--" she choked back more tears and struggled to keep her composure, "something that the whole youth group needs to hear."

Juliebeth was one of our most committed students. You could always count on her to show up. She wasn't the kind to complain about the cliques in our youth group either (I'm convinced some people really, really, desperately want there to be cliques so that they have an excuse not to come to things.). She is quiet, with a kind demeanor, and at the time wasn't someone I would've ever pegged to approach me after a lesson.

It wasn't hard to see the pain and hurt on Juliebeth's face as she spoke. The Word of God had ministered to Juliebeth's heart that night. It spoke to her, as it speaks to us: in a way that nobody else can, convicting the heart and calling for action.

I listened to Juliebeth's advice and quickly decided that she was right. I would share the message with the rest of the youth group.

We broke up into prayer groups and dismissed.

There was a very small handful of guys in the room that night, and I remembered that two of them, Chris and Alex, were first-time guests. I wondered how they might be feeling after a message like that. Did they think we had serious problems? Did they regret picking tonight to be the night that they would first attend?

Chris, Alex, a newer youth group guy named Will, and I made our way into a nearby classroom to pray. Aside from Will leading it, I honestly don't remember much about that prayer. But I'll never forget what took place afterwards.

I thanked the guys one last time for coming and was making my way towards the door when Chris interrupted.

"Hey."

"Hey, man. What's up?" I replied. Something was definitely on this guy's mind.

"Um...do you ever like...meet with people?"

I wasn't sure exactly what he meant by that question, but I pretended to and jumped at the opportunity. "Sure, man! Absolutely. I meet with people lots of times. Did you want to talk like, right now?"

"Well, I don't know." Chris hesitated then continued. "Yeah...I don't know why...but for some reason...I feel...like...maybe I should talk to you? But I'm not sure."

Somewhere inside of this guy's brain there was a Ping-Pong match happening.

"Hey, I don't want to pressure you at all, but I'm telling you, if you want to talk, let's talk, man. I'm happy to listen."

I led the way out of the youth dungeon and Chris followed me up the stairs. Before long we had settled into my office. We each found a seat around my desk, and I tried my hardest to listen with my ears and my heart, really having no idea what was coming.

"So, what's going on, man?"

There was a brief silence, and then Chris lost it. I mean **really** lost it.

He was sobbing, face buried in his hands, shaking, weeping. There was no consoling him.

We sat there a few minutes, but the only words spoken came in the form of tears. I didn't know exactly what was on his mind. The only thing I knew is that these were the same kind of tears that I had seen only moments ago in Juliebeth: tears of hurt.

. . . .

AN EXPERIMENT

It was February 24, 2012.

Every February, hundreds of youth ministers will tell you that they are going to take their groups to Challenge Youth Conference (CYC). The youth groups will tell you that they are going to Gatlinburg.

Ah, Gatlinburg. Every Southern child's dream. Where else can you go on earth that has more pancakes, go-karts, putt-putt golf, dinner shows, and pictures of Dolly Parton? That's right. Nowhere, that's where.

I know what you're thinking, "I **have** to go to that place."

Oh, but did I mention that Gatlinburg has nunchakus, ostrich jerky, and anything that could conceivably be sold featuring a wolf or an eagle on it? Because it does.

Still not ready to book your next vacation?

How many times have you thought, "I wish I had an airbrushed t-shirt of myself riding a dolphin," but gave up because you just didn't know where to find one? Look no further, my friend, than the City of the Three Smells: sweat, cigarettes, and fried.

I kid because I love Gatlinburg. I'm a sucker for it, too.

Each year CYC puts on a great program with some of the most powerful proclaimers of the Word of God you'll find anywhere. That year was no exception.

We had our regulars with us that year for CYC (I can only remember there being one guest), which worked out perfectly, because, if you remember, the regulars were the ones who missed Wednesday night's lesson about Esmin Green.

It was already dark when we finally made it to the mountains and settled into our cabin for our devotional. I opened up my Bible and delivered word for word the message I shared on Wednesday night, with the exception of one small thing that I added to this message. I concluded the message that night with this:

"Guys, as we wrap up tonight, let me share with you sort of a fear that I have. Here's what I fear. I think we can come here and say, "Yes! Let's do this! Let's put an end to the culture of neglect in our youth group! Let's help Esmin Green! We're going to be Jesus to everybody who walks through the doors of our building! From now on, things are going to be different!

"Listen guys, it's one thing to have a different weekend. It's another thing to go home and make things different. How are we going to know if things have really changed?

"How many of you know Chris and Alex?" *(I think one hand went up.)*

"Chris and Alex are two guys who came for the first time this past Wednesday night. In fact, how crazy is this? It was the first time either one of them had ever stepped foot inside of a church building! They had never even been inside of a church building.

"And so think about it, guys. Here are two guys that we have no connection with at all. They know Abbie Earhart who invited them, and that's it.

"You guys know what a control in a science experiment is? These two guys are literally the control in our experiment. How will we know if things are really different in our youth group when we get back home?

"Here it is: will we keep seeing Chris and Alex? That's it. Can these two guys 'make it' in our youth group. If we keep seeing them, then we know something's changed. But if not, nothing's changed."

. . . .

LEAVING THE CAFETERIA

I have been a part of some emotionally charged events before. Mission trips. Church camps. Retreats. You know the kind. The kinds of events where by the end of the day/night/weekend/week the entire group is ready to move to a third world country to do mission work.

Give people a week, and emotions die down. Emotional reactions are not always a bad thing. In fact, there's a lot right about those kinds of events and reactions. Emotion is good. Feeling is good.

In Acts 2, when God used Peter to make His plan of salvation clearly known for the first time to the people in Jerusalem, it ripped their hearts out. "Now when they heard this, they were cut to the heart and said to Peter and the rest of the apostles, 'Brothers, what shall we do?'" (Acts 2:37).

An emotional response is a natural response to the Word of God.

Then the people asked a simple question: "Brothers, what shall we do?"

Peter could've said, "You know what? It's pretty obvious that there are a lot of you who are saying that you want to be baptized, which I know is a super-popular thing to do right now. But let's face it: a lot of you are probably riding high on emotion. You are in no position to make this sort of decision right now. Why don't you guys sleep on it and then a few of us apostles will try to schedule a time where we can sit down and study with you in the next couple of weeks?"

An emotional reaction to the Word of God is good, but like I said, I've attended enough events to see that some reactions last just as long as the trip lasts.

I didn't want this to be one of those trips.

We had yet to determine whether or not we were going to be a different kind of youth group, but one thing was for sure: it certainly was a different kind of weekend. We shared more laughs, smiles, inside jokes, and hugs that weekend than we had at every other weekend combined since I had begun working at Mt. Juliet.

For the first time in a long time, I had fun.

It was like God had lifted a burden off everybody's chest.

We were free.

We left Gatlinburg different, but would we arrive in Mt. Juliet different? That was the thought that sort of haunted me all the way home. How do we make this stick? How do we keep from having to go back to the high school cafeteria, that cold, predictable atmosphere--a place you'd never go back and visit?

6

WE FEEL AWKWARD SO YOU DON'T HAVE TO!

THE ESQUAD

"Hey, Philip. Have you read this book?"

My eyes hadn't left my computer screen and I was already ready to answer her question, but I politely waited until she showed it to me.

"Hmmmm...*Sustainable Youth Ministry* by Mark DeVries. No."

If anyone else had given me a copy of that book, I probably would've taken it as if someone were offering me a breath mint because my breath was so terrible. "Hey, your ministry stinks. You really need this."

But that's not Tracie Shannon at all.

I knew this of course, which is why I naturally chose to respond with, "Is there something you're trying to tell me, Tracie?" She's fun to mess with.

Tracie laughed, "No!" She laughed and continued, "It's just that, well, my dad says this is the greatest book on youth ministry he's ever read, and so I thought I'd get you a copy if you didn't already have one!"

That was a high compliment coming from her dad. I didn't know him very well but I knew that he reads tons of books.

"Wow! Thanks so much!" I said, pretending to be someone who reads a ton of books.

Tracie laid the book down on the corner of my desk...where it went untouched for the next two or three months...you know...because... I...was...too busy finishing up the other 1,999 books I always read.

Perhaps the most remarkable part of the story that I'm about to share is that **I actually read it** (and maybe the highest compliment that I could give about the book is that it actually made me consider reading more books! I said, "consider").

For the record, the book is remarkable. Many of the concepts shared in that book helped form my ministry and gave it some much-needed structure and direction. Go buy it and read it.

One of the parts that especially stood out at me was something he mentions called the Extravaganza Squad (or ESquad for short).

> One of my greatest thrills over the past three years was having my son Adam on the staff of our youth ministry as the high-school outreach director. During his short tenure, he championed (loudly and repeatedly) the priority that everyone who walks through the door of our youth ministry feel loved. He accomplished this priority primarily through the creation of The Extravaganza Squad (or ESquad for short). Our Extravaganza Squad is a group of forty or so students who have taken as their responsibility the creation of a contagious friendship culture in every program of our youth ministry...
>
> The ESquad owns the atmosphere for every guest; they own the responsibility for making every outsider student in the room feel like a VIP. Every Sunday school class also has a mini ESquad that meets fifteen minutes before the students start to arrive. In these meetings, the group celebrates the ways outsiders have been made to feel welcome during the previous week, identifies any fringe students who might need a little special attention and prays together...

And I'm pretty sure this was the line that sold me on the concept.

> Somewhere in the first few meetings, the ESquad came up with a motto that captured this responsibility perfectly: "We feel awkward so you don't have to!" Each time the ESquad gathers...their most consistent ritual is "stacking it up"...and shouting in unison, "We feel awkward so you don't have to!"[3]

. . . .

LET'S DO LUNCH

"James! Hey, man! It's Philip. How you doing?"

"Oh, hey! Not too bad, man, not too bad. What's up?"

"Oh, dude, not too much. Just working a little bit. What are you up to?"

"Oh, nothing much. Just chillin' at home right now."

"Cool, cool. Hey, random phone call but the reason I was calling is because...well, did you see that text I sent out earlier about a meeting coming up this Wednesday night?"

"Uhhhhhh???"

"Ok, well there's a meeting coming up Wednesday night. It's about Esmin–"

"Oh, yeah! Esmin Green, the stuff that we talked about in Gatlinburg!"

"Yes, exactly! Well, the reason I was calling is because I need you there. You're a natural leader, and you are a guy that people listen to and follow, and I think it's going to be important for you to be at to this meeting. Do you think there's any way you can make it?"

---

[3] *Sustainable Youth Ministry* by Mark DeVries. "The Magnet Effect" p.166-167, 170.

"Yeah, man. I think I can make that work."

And James' answer was the same as 19 other high school students who assembled together for the first time at 6:00 p.m. on February 29, 2012, Leap Day. It would go on to be the very first of many what we would later call Lunch Ladies meetings.

The following is a copy of my manuscript from that meeting:

You're probably wondering why you're here tonight...let me begin by telling you another story.

There were two men. One of them was named Paul Revere. You've probably heard of Paul Revere's midnight ride, where he loudly cried out "The British are coming!" But what a lot of people don't know is that there was another man by the name of William Dawes who was given the same message as Paul Revere.

So two men were given the same message--to warn local militias to prepare for the British invasion that was coming in the morning. Those on the side of the river assigned to William Dawes heard the message and then rolled over and went right back to sleep.

But those alerted by Paul Revere sprung to life, with the warning spreading like wildfire to the surrounding villages and farms. The message was exactly the same, but the results couldn't have been more different.

So why did I ask you to show up tonight? I want you to know that I view each of you as Paul Reveres in a world full of William Dawes. In other words, I believe that you have the ability to influence the people around you in a good way. And I'm asking you to use your gift and your influence to create a revolution of authentic friendship in our youth group.[4]

---

[4] The William Dawes/Paul Revere story comes from *Sustainable Youth Ministry* by Mark DeVries. p.167-168.

I'm asking you to become a part of an unofficial team on Wednesday nights. Kind of like a special undercover task force. I won't say a lot about you guys publicly, because this isn't something that every single person in our youth group is going to be involved in. Remember, we're an undercover task force. We will operate under the radar. But I know that if the people inside of this room are on my team, together we can dramatically change the effect of our youth ministry here not just in this church, but in this entire city of Mt. Juliet!

And so here's what I'm saying: Every Wednesday night at 6:30 I'm going to ask you guys to come to this room, and here's what we're going to do. We're going to meet for about 20 minutes and we're going to do three things each week. So here are the three things that we'll do every week.

 Celebrate the good.

The first thing we're going to do is talk about the people we welcomed and reached the week before. So number one, we're going to celebrate the good.

To show you how this will work, let me tell you what I saw Spencer do last week. First of all, he was at the door (along with about 7 others of you) greeting people. Then after class, he hung around afterwards and talked the entire time to Chris (that guy that I told you about that had never been to church until two weeks ago).

Spencer wasn't being fake or weird; he was just being himself. He hung around Chris and Abbie the entire time until Chris, Abbie, and I left for a Bible study, at which time I said, "Hey, man, I'll see you later."

At the beginning of the Bible study I asked Chris how things were going and if he'd met anybody. He said, "Actually, yeah. I met Spencer tonight. He was really cool."

Same thing happened, by the way, with Taylor. She talked to Alex the entire time, made him sit with her, etc. So cool! A senior girl welcoming a freshman.

That's what I mean by celebrating the good. And guess what? You know what's going to happen to guests that come to our class and see how welcomed and appreciated that they are? They're going to come back.

And guess who's coming back again tonight? Alex and Chris.

2 *Identify people on the fringe.*

You know what I mean by people on the fringe, right? They come to class, but that's about it. They're just kind of standing on the sidelines watching the action, but they're not really in it.

Let's go ahead and see what this looks like. And by the way, the names we mention don't need to leave the room.

(We threw out a few names.)

3 *Finally, the third thing we will do each week is pray about what the group is setting out to accomplish that night.*

Again, we want every single person that walks into this room to feel welcomed. And that doesn't end just when he or she comes through the door. That means nobody sits alone. Nobody gets ignored. Everybody who comes inside of that room should be treated like Jesus. You guys with me?

Now, final business before we leave.

Two things. One, we will meet next week at 6:15 to evaluate how everything went. We may make more specific assignments; you guys may have some great ideas about something I haven't thought about. Who knows? But that's number one, we'll meet next week at 6:15 to talk about how everything went.

Two, before we leave, you guys need to name yourselves. I jotted down three names that I thought you guys might like, and we'll let you guys decide what you like the most.

Here they are, with a brief description of each name.

The Lunch Ladies. Remember my analogy about the high school cafeteria and how everybody has a specific section that they sit in? Well, if you think about it, the lunch ladies are about the only people inside of the cafeteria that associate with everybody, regardless of who you are or where you sit. They serve anybody and everybody. That's why I like that one. So there's option number one: you can be called the Lunch Ladies.

Another option: the Extras. Extras are the people that are in virtually every TV show or movie that work in the background. They are important, but few people really know just how much that they do. They exist to blend in by just doing their job.

The Zambonis. The Zamboni is the machine that comes out onto the ice before every hockey game and in between the periods. It comes out and smooths everything over. It takes care of the ice. It prepares the ice for play. When the Zamboni does its job, everybody wins. See the similarities there? If we come in and prepare the ice for the rest of the group, the environment will be just right.

Guys, I really feel like if we can get the environment right in here, we will be seeing a lot more people walking through those doors week after week and coming back! I'm excited to see how this group will work! Our next meeting will be at 6:15 next week. Let's pray.

(Bowed for prayer)

And finally, we're going to end each meeting every week with a team cheer. Here's how it goes. Ready? "1, 2, 3! We feel awkward so you don't have to!"

The Lunch Ladies were born.

7

DISCOVERING ELECTRICITY

THE NEW NORMAL

You could tell that things were different from the first moment that the Lunch Ladies entered our "cafeteria." If you weren't "in" on what was happening on that night and you were a regular, the scene had to look bizarre--so different in fact, that I wondered if the rest of the youth group would know something was up!

It was almost as if 20 of their peers had gotten together before class and conspired to make things more awesome or something...

The Lunch Ladies absolutely owned the room. They spoke to everybody, nobody sat alone, and they worked the entire crowd. This was no easy task considering the youth dungeon was engineered for about as much fun and fellowship as your local D.M.V. The room was so misshapen and overcrowded that the only way you could "work the room" was by crawling over people and positioning yourself awkwardly in chairs. Did I mention the chairs didn't move?

It almost provided an element of comic relief to me as I took in the scene. "We feel awkward so you don't have to" was definitely the perfect tagline for what I was watching.

And what I was watching was beautiful.

Needless to say, I went into the next week's Lunch Ladies meeting fired up. And guess who else was? The Lunch Ladies! They knew that they had killed it. And it felt good to be able to celebrate wins like that in a meeting together.

And the first Wednesday night was only the beginning: in the weeks that would follow, more and more students were following the Lunch Ladies' lead. No longer were students coming straight into a room and looking for a seat. They became people looking for people.

The atmosphere was changing: this was the new normal. This was the way that things were going to be.

As for that very small minority that decided they were too cool for everybody else (every youth group has them at some point), they began to quickly realize that their reign had come to an end and that their intimidation tactics (like being a snob or making fun of people) no longer held any sway. The subtle message was clear: that way wasn't going to be the way anymore.

This cafeteria was under new management, and now, the Lunch Ladies were in charge! (I'm picturing all the lunch ladies of America holding up their spatulas in victory, marching while "Mine Eyes Have Seen the Glory" plays in the background). We had taken the bullies' power away from them.

How? The Lunch Ladies decided it was more important to do the will of God than to worry about anything else.

Be a snob. Call them awkward. Make fun. It didn't matter. They were going to do God's work.

· ·

THE WALL

Nehemiah was a man with a great burden on his heart. When he heard the news about the wall in Jerusalem being destroyed, his heart broke. He looked at the way things were and he wanted something better.

He wanted to build something. Something important. A wall of protection.

But the burden on Nehemiah's heart was not for building a wall. The burden was for what the wall was being built for: a people. So there was Nehemiah, a righteous man who sought to do something wonderful for the Lord--build up a broken people.

Naturally, a couple of Bible bullies showed up. They were threatened at the very idea of anyone seeking the welfare of the broken people of Israel. Now whom would they bully?

"But when Sanballat the Horonite and Tobiah the Ammonite servant heard this, it displeased them greatly that someone had come to seek the welfare of the people of Israel" (Nehemiah 2:10).

But Nehemiah and the people pressed on, and the work continued. Sure they looked unusual (ever seen a construction worker carry a stack of 2x4s and a sword at the same time?!! Nehemiah 4:17-18), they weren't popular, and it was even scary at times, but to them God's work was more important.

God's work is more important than usual-ness. God's work is more important than popularity. God's work is more important than our fears.

Why? Because it's **God's** work.

I'm not sharing that Nehemiah story because I think I'm Nehemiah or because I think the students in our youth program who were resistant to what we were building are as evil as Sanballat and Tobiah. I share that story because we all need to be reminded of the fact that anytime we attempt to do something for God, we will meet opposition to the work.

But let us never forget: it is God's work. It is bigger than you or I. It is bigger than your biggest critic. It is bigger than a bunch of picketing idiots.

"When our enemies heard that it was known to us and that God had frustrated their plan, we all returned to the wall, each to his work" (Nehemiah 4:15).

Sometimes we see God frustrate the plans of those that oppose the work, but plans that are from God always come to pass.

. . . .

LET THERE BE LIGHT

For us, the beginning of Lunch Ladies was like discovering electricity. Everything changed. I'm not exaggerating. It was, and it is, the most unbelievable, most rewarding thing I've ever been a part of in ministry.

The Lunch Ladies story is one about what happens when God's light shines into a room: darkness is exposed, and light wins.

At the time of this writing (1/1/15):
- Our youth ministry has grown from 100 active students (2010-11 school year) to 203 active students (2014-15 school year) (Note: "active" means it is not uncommon for a student to attend at least one time per week.)
- There is rarely a week that goes by that we do not have a first-time guest come in for a visit.
- We have baptized 101 6th-12th graders into Christ since "The Day Indifference Died" back on February 22, 2012.
- The Lunch Ladies have gone from having 16 involved to nearly 40.
- Other versions of Lunch Ladies ministries have been started at congregations in Memphis, TN, Paragould, AR, and Frankfurt, KY.
- We have (finally!) left the youth dungeon and have a beautiful building that our youth ministry calls home.

I am continuously amazed at how much I learn from a group of righteously ticked-off high school students who demand to put an end to a culture of neglect and indifference.

Much like Israel needed Nehemiah and his workers to do their jobs, and much like Esmin Green needed a hospital and its workers to do their jobs, the world needs the church and its workers to do their job.

I'm thankful for the times that the church gets it right. Part Two of this book consists of a few of those such times: some success stories ("successipes") that I have chosen to share with you, each one communicating an important lesson learned from being part of this ministry.

To God be the glory.

PART 2
SUCCESSIPES

8

LIFE AND GODLINESS

THE RIGHTEOUS DARE

His face was still buried in his hands, and he hadn't said a word.

At the time, the only thing I knew about him was his name, Chris--well, that and the fact that he was sitting inside my office in an immense amount of pain.

After a few minutes Chris began to try and translate the tears.

"I-- I don't know. I-- I just..." More tears.

"Hey, it's okay, man. You take all the time you need. I'm listening."

"It's just-- when you were talking about how you felt in the 7th grade, I totally-- I mean, that just...really hit home for me."

More tears. And a little bit more of his story.

"You know, maybe, just maybe, you were here tonight for a reason," I said. "I mean how crazy is it we had that particular lesson that on the very first night that you and your brother ever stepped foot inside of a church building? I have a hard time calling that a coincidence."

And to think, I almost didn't use the Esmin Green lesson that night. I don't think using it was a coincidence either.

Honestly, when Chris left my office I wasn't sure if I'd ever see him again. I strongly encouraged him to come back the next week. We exchanged cell numbers, and I practically begged him to call me if he needed anything at all, at any time, any day.

Chris and his brother Alex were the two guys I mentioned in the lesson on the Gatlinburg trip after only meeting them two days before:

"Here are two guys that we have no connection with at all. They know Abbie Earhart who invited them, and that's it... These two guys are literally the control in our experiment...how will we know if things are really different in our youth group? Here it is: will we keep seeing Chris and Alex? That's it. Can these two guys 'make it' in our youth group. If we keep seeing them, then we know something's changed. But if not, nothing's changed."

Looking back, that was a pretty tall order, a pretty tough test to pass! But I guess God must've interpreted it as a "righteous dare." Perhaps that is what more of our prayers should look like.

We moved Chris and Alex's names to the top of our list (by the way, we refer to that list as "The Menu"), and they were on our radar every single week for the next year to year and a half. Chris, Abbie, and I met together in my office to study the Bible almost every Wednesday night for the next 3 months, and there wasn't a week that went by where those two guys weren't prayed for, not a week where one of the Lunch Ladies wasn't reaching out to them, inviting them over to their houses, out to eat, on retreats, even to church camp!

What happened was incredible: Chris and Alex, two guys who had never even been inside of a church building, haven't missed a single week since the first time they came (with the exception of a family vacation).

We had passed the test: things were really different after all.

. . . .

ATHEIST TO A THEIST

On the night that Chris first came to Mt. Juliet, he was seeking something--he just didn't know Who it was yet. As usual, God delivered on His promise: "For everyone who asks receives, and he who seeks finds, and to him who knocks it will be opened" (Luke 11:10, NKJV).

After a whole lot of asking questions, after a whole lot of knocking, after a whole lot of seeking, after leaving the youth group for college, after continuing to attend church, and after connecting with a Christian Student Center on his college campus, Chris, once an atheist, made the decision to follow Christ. What a joy to be the one to baptize him.

It was during one of our late night phone calls when Chris asked, "Have I ever told you why I decided to come to Mt. Juliet on that particular night?"

"No, I don't think so." I remembered him saying that he'd been invited by Abbie, but I guess I hadn't ever considered why he decided to come.

He said, "For me, it was either commit suicide or give church a try."

2 Peter 1:3 says, "His divine power has granted to us all things that pertain to life and godliness, through the knowledge of Him who called us to His own glory and excellence."

The simple way that I've come to translate this verse is that God gives us everything we need to know about life and how to live it (godliness). "His divine power" is the power that "granted to us" the Word of God, the Word that gives us knowledge of Him who called us. "His divine power" is also the same power that "granted to us" the gift of His Son, who gave us "knowledge of Him who called us to His own glory and excellence."

Jesus is the personification of what happens when life and godliness collide. He didn't just come to tell us how God wanted us to live our lives (there were a lot of hypocritical people doing that). He came to show us exactly how God would live our lives. He blazed a trail for us ("granted to us") back to the One "who called us to...glory and excellence."

To me what makes Chris' story so beautiful is that it illustrates the way in which God, in a way that only He can do (divine power), "grants to us" exactly what we need in "life;" and what we need in life, we eventually discover, is "godliness."

Chris had tried living his life without God, and what he discovered was the need for God in it. Godliness.

God was showing Himself to Chris by showing Chris His people at exactly the time when Chris understood his need for God the most.

When Chris needed a friend and a brother to be loved by, God gave him Zion.

When Chris needed someone to see his hurt, God gave him Abbie, a faithful, patient friend who extended the first invitation for Chris to meet Christ and His people.

When Chris needed to hear God's message of hope, God led him to a place he had never been before: a church building, where, on a Wednesday night inside of a cold, half-empty classroom, a message of hope was offered.

When Chris needed an older friend to listen, to pray, and to lovingly speak the truths of God's Word into his searching heart, God gave him a youth minister.

When Chris needed to be noticed, God gave him the Lunch Ladies.

When Chris needed some friends, God gave him 150 in the youth group, who instantly embraced him.

When Chris needed some closer friends in the youth group, God gave him Spencer, Kelsie and Mackenzie, Brenna, and a whole bunch more I'm leaving out.

When Chris needed to hear that there was a light at the end of the tunnel, God gave him David.

When Chris needed a philosophical thinker, God gave him John Michael.

When Chris needed to laugh, God gave him Todd.

When Chris needed to hear the Truth wrapped up in love, God gave him James.

When Chris needed someone to help him grow spiritually at his new home in college, God gave him Scott and a Christian Student Center full of support.

When Chris needed a family, God gave him the church.

When Chris needed saving, God gave him a Savior.

"You see, at just the right time, when we were still powerless, Christ died for the ungodly" (Romans 5:6, NIV).

9

THE LUNCH LADY I NEVER MET

PRAYER ROCKS

"Hey, man! How's it going?"

"................ummmmmmmmmm, gooooood?"

"Awesome! Any news?"

"................uhhhhhhhhhhhhhhhhhhhhhh.........noooooo?"

"Ok. Well, what's on your mind?" I asked.

I had gotten to know Alex pretty well over the course of the past year. Like I said, Chris and Alex, the two guys who had never been inside of a church building, hadn't missed a single week since they had first "mysteriously" (the Lord works in mysterious ways) showed up on the Wednesday night that changed everything.

Alex is two years younger than Chris, and to say that he is the quieter of the brothers would be a dramatic understatement. For the first several months that we were getting to know Alex, he never said more than one or two words in his answers to us (because we had to ask him questions to get him to speak).

Yet despite his silent demeanor, he quickly became a celebrity in the youth group, one of those kids everybody knew and everybody loved.

You can imagine my surprise when he asked if he could meet up with me in my office to talk about something.

"Ok, so what's on your mind?"

I prepared myself, not knowing what in the world was coming. I listened intently, ready for Alex to slowly, carefully unload a thought or two...or really, just one.

Nothing.

I studied Alex, trying to get some kind of read on him. He didn't move a muscle, eyes glued to the floor. I couldn't judge by the look on his face whether he'd just received word that he was moving to Afghanistan or if he'd won a new car. It was like trying to interpret the Mona Lisa. Lady Gaga couldn't read his poker face--I instantly regret making that joke.

I gave him a few seconds to respond before trying again.

"Hey, it's alright, man. You take all the time you need. I'm listening."

I waited...

And waited...

And waited...

Nothing.

I meant what I said, but if he really had "taken all the time that he needed," we might still be in my office.

I couldn't help but think back to the first time I met him. It was in those first few minutes before class on "Esmin Green" Wednesday. I walked over to him, stuck out my hand, and said, "Hey, I'm Philip! It's nice to meet you! I'm the youth minister here." He never looked up, half-heartedly shook my hand and said--you guessed it--nothing.

This was familiar territory.

"It's okay, Alex. Take your time. Whenever you're ready, I'm listening."

Still waiting for Alex to give me some sort of indication as to why we were meeting in my office, I had an idea. I stood up and turned around to take something off of my bookshelf.

"Do you remember this?"

I sat back down in my chair, and placed a small, white rock on my desk.

"............................yes," said Alex.

The white rock had Alex's name on it. He had given me that rock at church camp that summer. The assignment was for campers to write their names on a rock and give it to someone that they viewed as a rock, someone they could count on to offer up their names in prayer.

"Alex, I want you to know how much this rock means to me. But really it's not about what the rock means to me. It's the name on the rock, it's about what you mean to me. I can't tell you how much we love seeing you and Chris here all the time. You're like two of the most faithful attendees in our youth group. I mean, to me, it feels like you guys are family here. Everybody here loves you, and I'm so grateful that God brought you here."

I studied Alex again. He still hadn't moved, and he still hadn't said a word.

He was so quiet--in fact he was so still--that I almost didn't notice the tears streaming down his face. He was crying.

I'm not sure who was caught more off-guard by those tears: Alex or me.

I couldn't help but wonder when was the last time he had done that? I'll never forget those silent tears.

. . . .

PAPER COVERS ROCK

Alex was never able to verbalize what was on his mind that night. We ended our time with a prayer, and with my suggesting that he might try writing down what he wanted to say.

The following Wednesday night Alex handed me this note.

> *Hey, Philip. How are you doing? On Wednesday what I wanted to do was talk about some of my social problems to you. From the beginning I never was good talking to people because of a few things, such as I never could talk to anyone unless I was spoken to first, I never really had any reason to, and there usually was nothing for me to say since I sleep every day during the day (I don't sleep at night). I can only play video games on the weekend, and I don't really have much of a life since that's all that I normally do.*
>
> *When I went to school every day from preschool to 8th grade, I never had any friends to talk to, and it just always ended up me doing nothing every day for years. It's very boring to go to a place where I sat alone, did nothing, and watched everyone else talk. This always made me either extremely sad or very frustrated, but I never did want anyone to know about this, so I got rid of all my emotion.*
>
> *People have told me I can keep a good straight face since they've never seen me smile, laugh, or mad in their entire lives. Some teachers have told me, "Wow. I didn't expect you to still be here. All you ever did was nothing."*
>
> *My 8th grade award (it's something that everyone gets that describes them) was for having no emotion, never smiling, and having a straight face. The reason people had for me not talking to them was that I hated everybody.*
>
> *One day I actually got very sick with a rare disease when basically the main problem was that there was a lot of mucus that*

started to accumulate to the point I would choke and die. I was stuck in a hospital for about a week. Then when I got back to school nobody knew where I had been. Also no one really cared.

But when I'm at church and I miss one day, I get five people asking me where I am.

School was something that always made me depressed to go to since I never had a place to go. I was always alone, doing nothing, waiting to get out. And I had all this bottled up inside for years. And all of this happened just because I couldn't talk to people. It may seem simple but it never was for me.

Eventually when I was a freshman, one day at the beginning of the year, I was doing nothing as usual when a girl walked in front of my desk and started to talk to me about who I was and who she was. And she started to do this every day and sometimes she brought her friends.

And for once I actually had friends at school.

One day she invited me to go to her church, almost exactly around the time Chris got invited to your church. We went to your church first since he got an address and I got a general location, but after hearing that first lesson and how everyone welcomed me I decided to stay with this one, so I never did go to hers though. And for once I had somewhere to go after school and I actually enjoyed school.

Now that I'm in 10th grade, I no longer have any classes with them since they're all juniors and I rarely ever see them any more. And now I'm back to just being myself doing nothing every day. I just don't really want this to happen again of how I felt when I was a kid, so I decided I would talk to you. But that didn't work out too well. Then I decided to write this paper. Sorry if this didn't make sense.

. . . .

AMAZING GRACE

The next time I heard about her was probably a year later. It was a late night after a youth event. I was taking Alex home and we had a few minutes (for me) to talk.

"So, I've got a question for you, man. All those months ago, on the first night that you came to Mt. Juliet, what was it that made you decide, 'You know, I think I'll go to church tonight'? Was it the fact that Chris was already going and you were like, 'Hey, why not? I guess I'll go, too,' was it that you were bored, or was it like for some other reason?"

There was the standard three-second pause, the one I fall for every time, where I convince myself that Alex didn't hear me or understand me correctly, and then he laid this on me.

"Well, basically, there was this girl named Grace who used to talk to me every day five minutes before class would start. She would ask me how my day was, how I was doing, and stuff like that. She was really nice to me.

"And...so...well...basically...Grace...she was a Christian...and so I decided that I wanted to meet more people like her. And when I found out Chris was going, that's when I decided to go, too."

Today, Alex is a Christian.

Why?

Because of grace, and because of Grace.

Only God could write a story so beautiful.

I'm thankful that a girl I've never met took the time to show Jesus to Alex, because we would've never met him if she hadn't. And if we had never met him, I have to wonder, where would he be? Would Alex be a Christian? I know there's no way for any of us to know that answer, but looking at the evidence, I'd have to lean towards a strong no.

The difference that Grace has made has not only changed Alex's life, it has changed Alex's forever. What Grace did will echo into eternity.

Alex's story screams a simple truth: **There is no substitute for the simple, iconic, unmistakable, authentic love of Christ**.

"By this all people will know that you are My disciples, if you have love for one another" (John 13:35).

It's so simple. It was done that way on purpose.

Jesus loves Grace. Grace loves Jesus. Grace shows Jesus' love to Alex. Alex sees something in Grace, who is a Christian. Alex wants to meet more Christians, and those Christians (who don't even know Grace) show Alex that same love that he was drawn to in the first place. It's not called "the love of Christians." It's called "the love of Christ."

Alex was not drawn to Grace, nor to Grace's own amazing ability to love people that she had in and of herself. Alex was drawn to "the love of Christ."

We must remember that the little things in life that we do, like talk to someone we don't know very well for five minutes, are not little things at all.

On the night when Chris and Alex first came, I handed everybody an index card with two questions for them to answer:

1 WHO IS YOUR ESMIN GREEN?

2 WHAT ARE YOU GOING TO DO ABOUT IT?

I'm not sure I had ever considered it before typing this sentence, but God was the One asking those two questions to our youth group.

Esmin Green was Chris and Alex.

What were we going to do about it? I'm thankful that our answer became "whatever it takes."

. . . .

We were almost to Alex's house when he asked me a question that melted my heart.

"Heyyyyyyyy. Do you think you could...well...I've got this friend on Xbox Live and...I don't really know what to say to him...so do you think you could pray for my friend on Xbox Live? I wanted to see about talking to him about God. I think he believes in God, but I don't know for sure...so...yeah...I...was...just...thinking that there are probably a whole lot of people out there like me...so...yeah."

How beautiful is that? Now Alex is the one concerned with doing the things Christians do. Alex is looking for Alexes.

How do people meet Jesus?

It usually doesn't happen on the road to Damascus. The way most people are going to meet Christ is by meeting a Christian.

Chances are, somebody showed Jesus to you. To whom will you show Jesus?

10

THE COURAGE FOR FAITH

PILLS BURY

I'll never forget the first time I met Tanner.

"Look, man, before we talk I gotta give you something, a'ight?"

"Ok," I replied, not knowing what was coming next.

As Tanner leaned into his chair and reached deeply into his pocket, I gave a quick "Am I about to get shot?" glance over to Emilie, the one responsible for bringing this guy into my office. The look on her face didn't rule out that possibility.

It didn't take long for Tanner to retrieve whatever it was that he was looking for, and now I was looking at it: a Ziploc bag of pills.

He dropped it on my desk, slumped back into his seat, looked me straight in the eyes and asked, "Can you get rid of these?"

I didn't think he was asking me to ingest them, so I said "Yeah," trying to pretend like my daily youth ministry routine consisted of taking narcotics off the streets.

"My friend gave these to me today to sell, but I don't wanna do this anymore."

IF YOU CAN'T HEAR IT, IT DOESN'T MATTER

It was in the beginning of Emilie's senior year of high school when she sat down with her dad to share some life-changing news.

"Dad, I had a realization," she began.

"Hey, Sweetheart. What's going on?"

"Ok, well, you know how all these years I've gone to school and I've just been like super-quiet and haven't really talked to people?"

Of course David knew that, but he wasn't exactly sure where this was going; maybe he expected an "I should just drop out of school" pitch.

"Uh huh," he replied.

"Well, I realized I can't bring people to Christ unless I befriend them first," she continued. "And that means I have to talk to them. Before I never talked to people at school because it's way out of my comfort zone. So I decided this year to talk to people that I'd gone to school with my whole life but had never talked to."

It's hard to read Emilie's words and not think about how simple and basic that sounds. You say, "Wait--you mean she called a family meeting with her dad to tell him that she had made a life-changing decision to talk to people?"

Yes.

Emilie continued, "And these people gave me the craziest looks but it was so worth it! I sort of turned it into a game and just laughed at their reactions. And, Dad, you want to know what the craziest thing about all of this is?"

"What's that?" David replied.

"When I started doing that to please God and bring others to Him, I ended up enjoying school so much more!"

. . . .

TANNER + FAMILY = FULL HOUSE

I wasn't sitting inside the classroom when the conversation took place, but it happened something like this.

Emilie was talking to her mom on the phone during school (gasp!), but before you send her to prison, you ought to know that she had a crisis that she was dealing with: what she wanted her mom to cook for dinner.

A half-asleep, wise-cracking, 12th grade boy trying to spit his best game to the 12th grade girl with the incredible singing voice who sits in front of him overhears and says, "Hey, tell your mom I'm coming to eat at your house tonight."

Tanner expected the same reaction he got whenever he made most of those kinds of jokes to a girl--her rolling her eyes and saying something to the effect of "in your dreams."

Imagine his surprise when Emilie said, "Okay. Hey, Mom, Tanner's coming to dinner tonight."

"Who?"

That night Emilie's family had a guest at their dinner table, and according to Tanner, the food was as good as Emilie had advertised.

. . . .

THE ORIGINAL LUNCH LADY

The day Tanner decided to hand over a bag of pills to me paled in comparison to the day on March 13, 2013, when Tanner decided to hand over his life to Jesus Christ.

Watching him grow over the years has been such a joy to witness. He's real, he's raw, he's outspoken, and he's passionate. He's been through more than I could possibly share in this book. He's had moments of great triumph and moments of great tragedy. He's a fighter with a fiery, young faith that I find myself admiring.

What's interesting about Tanner's story, and the reason that I chose to share it, is that it doesn't focus on the power of a group. Tanner's story illustrates what can happen when one Christian has the conviction and the courage to step out in faith.

> One of the two who heard John speak and followed Jesus was Andrew, Simon Peter's brother. He first found his own brother Simon and said to him, "We have found the Messiah" (which means Christ). He brought him to Jesus. Jesus looked at him and said, "You are Simon the son of John. You shall be called Cephas (which means Peter)" (John 1:40-42).

> One of His disciples Andrew, Simon Peter's brother, said to Him, "There is a boy here who has five barley loaves and two fish, but what are they for so many?" Jesus said, "Have the people sit down." Now there was much grass in the place. So the men sat down, about five thousand in number. Jesus then took the loaves, and when He had given thanks, He distributed them to those who were seated. So also the fish, as much as they wanted (John 6:8-11).

Andrew the apostle was the original Lunch Lady.

Andrew had a habit of bringing whomever he could find to Jesus. The first person he brought to Jesus was his brother Peter. I'd say that worked out okay. Peter went on to preach the first Gospel sermon in its entirety in Acts 2, and as a result of God's message that day, 3,000 souls are added to the church (Acts 2:41).

But answer me this: How many people did Andrew lead to the Lord?

One more than Peter.

Andrew was also the apostle responsible for bringing a small boy's Happy Meal to Jesus. As a result Jesus performed a miracle. Think of all the people (and the meals!) that Andrew served, fed, and reached just by having a heart that desired to show people Jesus.

When we have the courage to do something because of our faith, look what happens: God provides the increase. It happened with Andrew. It happened with Emilie.

It takes serious courage, patience, and love to bring your raw, unedited, blunt brother to the Lord, and it takes serious courage to think that something like a small meal could really make that much of a difference. That sentence is true of both Andrew and Emilie.

From time to time, Tanner brings up the day we first met...and from time to time I bring up how glad I am that he didn't shoot me.

11

THE POWER OF AN INVITATION

EXPIRATION DATE

He had been trying to work up the courage to ask her out for the last two years.

He was scared to death that she'd say no. They were really close friends. What if she started acting all weird around him? Asking her out could potentially change everything.

He'd dropped subtle hints to her before about dating, but he wasn't sure if she even picked up on them. Come to think of it, she had dropped a few hints of her own...hadn't she? He couldn't be sure, but one thing was for sure: he was listening.

He was listening while she described some of the horrible dates she had been on. He was listening when she talked about the things that different guys did that bug her. And you better believe he was listening when she described the perfect date.

That's exactly what he wanted to give her. There was a lot riding on this.

But even scarier than her saying "No" was the possibility of her saying "Yes."

What if she actually agreed to go out with him? That could be even worse! Talk about a disaster waiting to happen! What if the date bombed? What if the place he was taking her was really boring? Or worse, what if the date was so horribly bad that she'd never speak to him again? He didn't want to lose a friendship over this, and he knew all it would take is one bad date to ruin everything he had worked so hard for in this relationship.

. . . .

THE KINGDOM OF HEAVEN IS LIKE A DATE

What you've just read is a parable about the unspoken fears that people have about inviting a close friend to come with them to church for the first time.

Inviting someone to church makes us all feel a little vulnerable.

Some have been trying to work up the courage to ask a friend to come to church with them for years. They're scared to death to bring up the subject of church. What if they start acting weird? Inviting them to church could change everything, and we're not so sure we want that. It's easier to avoid that conversation altogether.

And then there's the small part of us that hopes our friend says "No." It's easier that way. A "No" doesn't cost us anything. It's the equivalent of running into that old friend from high school out in public and saying, "Hey, we should catch up sometime!" Neither one of you really wants to do that, nor do you have any intention of doing that once you leave Panera Bread. It's really just a polite "No," something you say because the idea of it sounds nice and sort of makes you feel like a good person.

You've dropped subtle hints before about church, but you weren't so sure they "got it." Your friend has even talked about some of the horrible experiences they have had with church.

But the scariest thought of all? What if they say actually "Yes," and it's an absolute disaster?

What if the speaker says something that is hurtful?

What if the Truth is not spoken in love?

What if that on that day when they do finally decide to come, it becomes a situation of the "worse-case-sermon scenario?" What if that one subject is brought up that just so happens to be the absolute worst subject that the preacher could have mentioned on the day your friend came for the first time? You know how that will go over.

What if it's boring?

What if nobody speaks to them?

What if the church experience is so terrible and horrible that your friend just shuts down afterwards, and he won't talk to you about his spiritual life at all? You don't want to lose a friendship over this, and all it would take is one bad church experience to seemingly ruin everything you had worked so hard for in that relationship.

I hate to say it, but I get it--I can understand that fear.

What if that friend that you have prayed for, that friend that you have invested in, that friend that has just been so opposed to the idea of God, finally opens up his heart to the point at which he is interested in seeing "what this whole church thing is about."

So they come. And nobody speaks to them. I mean **nobody**.

. . . .

AN ACTSMOSPHERE

If I have just described to you the church environment in which you find yourself, I plead with you to consider the church of the New Testament. What would it have been like to visit that church? Was it cold, rigid, and boring, or warm, loving, and exciting?

In the books of Acts, we can read about the kind of atmosphere the church was designed to have, one that I would describe as an "Actsmosphere."

> And they devoted themselves to the Apostles' teaching and the fellowship, to the breaking of bread and the prayers. And awe came upon every soul, and many wonders and signs were being done through the Apostles. And all who believed were together and had all things in common. And they were selling their possessions and belongings and distributing the proceeds to all, as any had need. And day by day, attending the temple together and breaking bread in their homes, they received their food with glad and generous hearts, praising God and having favor with all the people. And the Lord added to their number day by day those who were being saved (Acts 2:42-47).

There are more places we could look in the book of Acts (like the entire book!) for a more comprehensive list of characteristics, but in these verses we can see that the Actsmosphere is loving, selfless, sacrificial, united, devoted, fellowship-filled, believing, filled with awe, together, need-meeting, glad, generous, praising, favorable, evangelistic, and growing.

The church came not with boredom, but with power. It started with a bang--well, more accurately--a sound like a mighty rushing wind. Men began speaking in languages they'd never studied before (Acts 2:1-12), and it caused a scene. People started to notice, wondering aloud what was going on.

How can we miss it? From the beginning of its existence, the Spirit was meant to fill the church (Acts 2:38), and thereby, the atmosphere in and around the church is affected. The Spirit affects Christians (individually and collectively) from the inside out. The book of Acts shows us that the church ought to be a spectacle--not one that draws attention to herself, but a lamp stand for the One who will draw all people to Himself: Jesus Christ.

God wanted to create an Actsmosphere and so, that's **exactly** what He created.

I wish you could imagine what it would have been like to invite a friend on a retreat with you before the Lunch Ladies existed (maybe some of you don't have to imagine because you are living it). Inviting a guest was a very "hit or miss" experience. They might be spoken to, but probably not, and so they would probably only hang out with that one friend who invited them. When that happens the pressure is really on that friend to make sure that the guest he or she brought has a good time, and so he or she is left feeling like a babysitter.

But imagine bringing a friend on a retreat where there's not an atmosphere of indifference but an atmosphere of Acts 2. How is that friend treated?

Could you see how evangelism would take place in an Actsmosphere? Do you see how natural it becomes when everything you are and everything you do and everybody that's involved are about souls?

When an atmosphere of indifference becomes an Actsmosphere, church becomes a whole lot more (get ready to cringe) **fun**.

The churchy words (if you prefer) are joy and gladness.

Why are we so afraid of the word *fun*? Who invented the crazy idea that church isn't supposed to be fun? It's not the primary reason that the people of God come together, but it's a byproduct of the people of God coming together.

God invented fun. If church is a fun place to be, it's a good thing. If someone goes to church and they have fun (gasp!) and they like it (double gasp!), it doesn't mean they've sinned.

Apparently there was something David enjoyed about worshipping the Lord with other people. Psalm 122:1 records, "I was glad when they said to me, 'Let us go to the house of the Lord!'"

. . . .

THE FORGOTTEN FIRST STEP

From an early age, I was introduced to "the steps of salvation." There are probably a lot of you that can rattle them off faster than I can (hear, believe, repent, confess, be baptized), and can give me book, chapter, and verse for each item.

I have to say though, that I think there's a forgotten "first step" in that list.

The first step is an invitation. Nobody hears the Gospel without it.

Our students have come to realize that every time we host an event, be it a retreat, or church camp, or a Fwednesday, or what have you, it's not just an opportunity to bring a friend, but an invitation to change someone's forever.

One of my very favorite things to do in ministry is to look back on how God has been at work in the lives of our students, and how He's worked through invitations to events.

A freshman girl in our youth group named Brooke decided to invite a girl she played softball with to come on our fall retreat, and so we met Brice for the very first time. Brice fell in love with God's people, the church, and the following January, Brice became a Christian.

A freshman guy named Daniel invited his friend Ryan from school to come to church. Nine months later, Ryan became a Christian.

Melina invited a guy at her school named Andrew to come to church. A few short months later, Andrew was baptized into Christ.

On a spring retreat, a freshman in our youth group named Spencer invited a guy from his school named Christian to come with him. Christian came on the retreat, and he fell in love with God's people, the church. He went back home and said, "Mom, Dad, I found our new church home."

Christian came home and invited his parents and his two brothers, Patrick and Frazier, to come to church with him.

Fast forward the clock a few months, and Christian became a Christian.

Fast forward the clock a few weeks and Frazier became a Christian.

And fast forward the clock a few more weeks and Patrick became a Christian.

We met Nicole two months ago for the first time. She is from Ecuador and attends a high school where none of our students attend. Her parents don't go to church with us. But someone told her about a church a few miles down the road that loves people. And the rest is history: last night, praise God, I baptized Nicole into Christ.

Another one of my favorites came full circle today at the time of this writing.

Two and a half years ago, after pushing our students hard to invite their friends to come on our spring retreat (they always do such a good job with that), one of our high school boys named Matt answered the call and invited his friend Ruben to come with him.

Matt got sick on Friday before we left and didn't come with us. He didn't tell Ruben (what are friends for, right?). Ruben came anyway. I repeat: he was invited by a friend who didn't show up, he still came, and he loved it. And everybody loved him.

And over the next two and half years, we would see Ruben regularly, as he built friendship after friendship with the students in the youth ministry.

Tonight, I baptized Ruben, this kid we were "never supposed" to meet, into Christ. Praise be to God.

And so I ask you, how did that happen? How did Brice become a Christian? How did Ryan, and Andrew, and Christian, and Patrick, and Frazier, and Nicole, and Ruben, and on and on and on?

It all started with an Actsmosphere. And once the culture was right, an invitation was given.

God works through invitations.

Invitations to come to a place where they can belong and be loved. A place with people who laugh together, cry together, have fun together, share life together, and serve the Lord together. You see, we're drawn to this kind of thing because we're wired for this kind of thing: it's the church.

In Matthew 22, Jesus tells a powerful story about invitations.

> The kingdom of Heaven may be compared to a king who gave a wedding feast for his son, and sent his servants to call those who were invited to the wedding feast, but they would not come (Matthew 22:2-3).

"Well, God, I tried. I really tried. I invited a friend. But they didn't want to come."

"Okay," God says, "you did your part. You tried. And that's really all you can do. Let's do the feast anyways, with the regulars. Besides we'll still have over 50 people there."

No. That's not what God does at all. In fact, He does the opposite.

> [Then he] said to his servants, "The wedding feast is ready, but those invited were not worthy. Go therefore to the main roads and invite to the wedding feast as many as you find." And those servants went out into the roads and gathered all whom they found, both bad and good. So the wedding hall was filled with guests (Matthew 22:8-10).

God says, "Ok, new plan. Go invite people until you get a yes. Go everywhere. Good people, bad people, as many as you can find. Bring them. I want them to meet My Son."

God puts an invitation in our hands, but so many times, we talk ourselves out of inviting people.

Why?

"What if it's boring? What if they hate it? What if they hear something that they don't agree with?"

"Well, the person that I'm thinking about inviting--they're not a good person." (Remember the servants in the parable invited the "bad" people, too.)

"Well, you know, having to hang out with that person all weekend long--that's just going to get annoying."

"They already go to church somewhere, so it'd be a waste."

"I'll have to entertain them. And I like to go on retreats and relax."

Listen, God's servants are not the ones who get to decide who's on His guest list. God is the host, and the party is not about us. It is for His Son.

12

MORE THAN YOU THINK

OUT OF IDEAS

Aubrey was a girl that we had been trying to win for Christ for years.

It was hard, and she was sort of hard to read, hard to get to know. I think it's safe to say that at one point or another, all hands had been on deck in trying to reach this girl: her family, me, Laura, our Cocoon (what we call our small group ministry) Leaders, our interns, and, obviously, the Lunch Ladies.

In fact, the Lunch Ladies, for an entire month, thought really outside the box and hatched an elaborate, covert scheme to do something special for her every week for a month--even sending her a plush of her favorite animal with an anonymous note just to try to brighten her day!

But while I'm sure she appreciated it, we weren't sure if our efforts were doing anything to lead her closer to Christ. A great investment was made, yet even though there was consistent, but not overwhelming, dialogue with Aubrey about her decision to become a Christian, it didn't feel like we were making any progress.

We had worked just about every single angle we could think of, and we were out of ideas. All we knew to do was love and encourage her, offering up prayers on her behalf.

. . . .

Braxtin was one of the first guests I met when I began working at Mt. Juliet.

I met Braxtin his freshman year (before Lunch Ladies existed), when he came on the very first fall retreat that I directed. He was a freshman in high school at the time, and in the years that would follow he would become one of our most frequent guests.

Braxtin is one of those people that everybody loves. It doesn't matter if you're 12 or 52, he will become your friend by the end of the time that you're done talking to him. He has that natural charisma, likability, and personality. He is easy-going, fun loving, respectful, humble, and also has a great sense of humor (one reason we have always gotten along well).

It didn't take long for Braxtin to become a frequent name mentioned in our Lunch Ladies meetings. In fact, he may be the "leading scorer" when it comes to prayers for a specific individual in our youth group-- not because we love him the most, but because of the sheer amount of time he was on our prayer list without becoming a Christian: four years!!!

We had worked just about every single angle we could think of. We were out of ideas. All we knew to do was love and encourage him, offering up prayers on his behalf.

. . . .

OUT OF THE BLUE

And then one day out of the blue, I received a phone call from Aubrey's dad, asking if I could meet them at the church building: Aubrey had decided to be baptized into Christ.

And one day "at the buzzer" on the night of our "Senior Recognition Day," Braxtin was baptized into Christ by his best friend, James, another senior (an original Lunch Lady) who was the friend responsible for inviting Braxtin to come on that first retreat.

Braxtin waited a long time to become a Christian, but he made the most of every opportunity God gave him that summer. He led his first and second devotional (he did his first one the week after he became a Christian) and was a camp counselor with the freshmen boys. In fact, he was the only senior from that class that took on the responsibility of being a counselor. How fitting that Braxtin would take hold of the opportunity to influence the guys who were the same age that he was when he first started getting involved with the church.

And to top it all off...

Braxtin, now a freshman in college at Tennessee Tech University, is heavily involved in a campus ministry and sent me the following text just this past week: "Just out of complete curiosity, can you give me a tiny bit of info on summer internships there?"

I honestly cannot think of a better candidate for a youth ministry intern.

. . . .

FROM THE LUNCH LADIES' LIST TO THE LAMB'S BOOK OF LIFE

When I first heard the news that Aubrey and Braxtin had decided to follow Jesus, it caught me completely off guard.

Why?

Why does it surprise us when these types of things happen when we've been praying about them?

The reality is these types of things happen when we've been praying about them!

God has always capitalized on the moments when we run out of ideas. Perhaps, we should forego our ideas first, and begin by inquiring of Him. We shouldn't turn to God when we're out of ideas. Turning to God should be our first idea.

One of my favorite passages from the Bible is Ephesians 3:20-21, and these two verses could very easily be considered "theme verses" for Lunch Ladies.

"Now to Him who is able to do immeasurably more than all we ask or imagine, according to His power that is at work within us, to Him be glory in the church and in Christ Jesus throughout all generations, for ever and ever! Amen" (Ephesians 3:20-21, NIV).

A few weeks ago I heard Matt Vega say of those verses, "Have you ever considered the fact that God can do more than you think?" I love that.

Coming to a clear understanding of this passage, and of the mighty God that we serve, ought to cause us to pray.

Why? Because our God can do a whole lot more than you or I can ever think!

There's no telling how many names have gone from our prayer list into the Lamb's Book of Life. I say that not to boast in ourselves, but to boast in "Him who is able to do immeasurably more than all we ask or imagine, according to His power that is at work within us, to Him be the glory in the church and in Christ Jesus throughout all generations, for ever and ever! Amen."

So what about you? Have you "given up" on people because you're out of ideas on how to reach them? God can do more than you think. So pray...and don't be surprised when something more than you think happens! God is working, and He's working in grander ways than you or I can even begin to describe, recognize, or fathom.

. . . .

Two months ago I sat down to do a Bible study called *Take Route* with a freshman in our youth group named Joseph. The study is designed to lead people on a journey towards Christ. At the very end of the study, Joseph decided that he wanted to become a Christian. We also talked that day about how God has given Christians the responsibility to share His message with others--saved people save people.

"Who is someone that you'd like to help lead to the Lord?" I asked Joseph.

He paused, thought deeply for a few seconds, and responded with "C.J." You could tell from the look on his face that Joseph was sure about his answer and serious about his mission.

C.J. had only been at Mt. Juliet for a couple of weeks. Nobody really knew him, and he really didn't know anybody in the church, but that was about to change. All we knew is that he had come from a tough background, and the Lord had brought him our way.

"That sounds awesome," I replied. "C.J. could use a connection here, and I definitely think you could reach him. I tell you what, I'll be praying about that, and you be praying about that, and we'll see what happens."

Last night, out of the blue, C.J. walked forward during the song of encouragement at church.

I had no idea he was going to do that. And neither did Joseph.

"I want to be baptized," he said.

I had no idea he was going to do that. And neither did Joseph.

"...and I want Joseph to baptize me," he said.

I had no idea he was going to do that. And neither did Joseph.

And so last night, Joseph got the opportunity to do something more than he asked or imagined: he baptized his friend C.J. into Christ.

These types of things happen when we've been praying about them.

More than you think.

More than you ask.

More than you imagine.

13

IN THEIR OWN WORDS

I know that the Lunch Ladies touched the lives of many in and around our youth group, but I also saw a lot of change in me. I see people as souls now. My perspective has been changed, turned inside out to see the needs of others. I'm not the same person that I was and I'm thankful for that. The Lunch Ladies kicked me out of my comfort zone and held me accountable for showing God's love to **everyone**. *I gave more of myself, and God filled me up more in return. I am full because the Lunch Ladies helped me to empty myself into others.*
— Rebecca, Lunch Lady 2012-2014

On the night Philip presented the Esmin Green story to the youth group in Gatlinburg, people's hearts opened up and tears were shed. I can remember staying up till almost four o'clock in the morning talking with girls from my grade because we had all felt left out or alone at one time…we were a completely different group of people.

One of the biggest changes I noticed was in myself. I was no longer afraid to talk to people from different grades or once before considered cliques. I was no longer worried about who I would sit with because I was more concerned about who others would end up sitting with. I became so focused on how others felt about the youth group and themselves that I no longer cared about what others thought about me.

No one ever deserves to feel alone because that's one of the worst feelings in the world. Everyone in Lunch Ladies was determined to make sure that would never happen to anyone.

I noticed it not just at church--I was able to talk to strangers/ newcomers--but at school as well. I became comfortable with asking people whom I hardly knew to come to church with me. In fact everyone in the youth group started bringing more people with them. Some of the people today that are constantly involved with the group were strangers or newcomers at one time. If Spencer had never invited Christian and Kelsie to church, then we would have never had our family. Who would have known that hanging out with two strangers on the spring retreat would lead to some of the closest people I now have in my life.

I am beyond grateful for what Lunch Ladies has done for the youth group and my life.

—Juliebeth, Lunch Lady 2012-2014

. . . .

I remember the day I walked into the first meeting. I was one of the youngest ones there, having just turned fifteen. It was the February of my freshman year in high school. The second I heard the idea behind the name "Lunch Ladies," I became excited. All my life, I had been someone who wanted to make people feel welcome and loved. To have a whole group whose main purpose was to do reach the unloved thrilled me.

As time went on, our meetings continued to change. They grew in time, and they grew in productivity. One thing I always noticed about the meeting was how the people who were a part of the group very easily could recognize when someone was hurting. I had this ability as well, but did not notice my ability as much as I noticed others. This helped me to grow into a stronger leader. I strived to be more like those who were caring about others and who had the courage to go speak to those they didn't know that night in class.

Lunch Ladies grew me into the young man I am today. Now, I am a senior, and I continue to take part in the group. We now have a much larger group with many people who are younger than me. Our youth group at the Mt. Juliet church of Christ has grown tremendously, and *probably a large portion of it has been because of God working through the Lunch Ladies. As I've gotten older, I have found it difficult to remember all the names of the kids even just three years younger than me. Thankfully, we are the church, and we have many members. The Lunch Ladies have the unique ability to be those leaders who know everybody. Even though I may not know everyone, the powerful thing about the Lunch Ladies is there is always someone who knows the one needing to be reached.*

God has blessed me so much to be a part of this group. Had I not gotten to be a part of it, I have no idea where I would have been today. As I've grown the last four years in maturity, I have come to realize that this work for God is so much more powerful than I ever anticipated. The young guy sitting in that meeting in 2012 would've never imagined the growth that would come from it. Lunch Ladies has truly helped save souls.

—Ben, Lunch Lady 2012-2015

. . . .

It's weird to see how much everything has changed, and in a way it makes me feel older than I really am, or maybe I'm just finally realizing my age. Either way, things are still different for the people here than they were when I first started out my freshman year as one of the first Lunch Ladies.

I remember that first meeting, the text Philip sent to me. I remember my friend Megan, and I remember all of the confused faces meeting upstairs in one of the top rooms for the first time wondering what crazy thing Philip had thrown together this time. It took a while before he finally came in, but when he did the first meeting took place.

The Lunch Ladies is a tool God uses to help the youth group grow and prosper. As the youth group changes, the Lunch Ladies change too. New members come in, and old members fade away--some because they graduate, and others for other reasons, but it's been a blessing to have been able to come in from the beginning and to graduate from it in the end. It is hard to imagine how things in my life might have been *if Lunch Ladies didn't exist, if I would still be close to some of the same people. And though it's changed and we've changed, one thing should always remain the same: Lunch Ladies should always be a tool for God and should always be a blessing to everyone.*

—Abbie, Lunch Lady, 2012-2015

. . . .

Being a part of the Lunch Ladies ministry was an experience that has transformed the way I view social interaction within the church. As a high schooler, I had been on both sides of the spectrum, having friends and feeling welcome as well as feeling alone and uncomfortable. At the time, I didn't realize how powerful it was to simply make a visitor (or even a member) feel welcome. As the Lord's church, we are called to reach out to others, regardless of social norms and expectations. This ministry really opened my eyes to see the need to reach out to people, especially when they may not be familiar or close with anyone present.

I also am reminded of the initial video we saw that really spurred the founding of the LL ministry: the story of Esmin Green, a lady who came to the E.R. but was denied help for so long that she died in the waiting room. I remember our discussion being that she came to the very place that was designed to help her, but they did not provide it. As the church, we are designed to help our neighbors, whether they are physically ill or sitting alone on a pew. If we deny help to those that come to us for that very reason, then how are we loving our neighbors?

Basically, it doesn't matter who the person is or how he/she looks–each person is valued by God and that should matter to us. I will forever be grateful for this ministry and how it has taught me to seek out those who are in need of a friend.

—Claire, Lunch Lady 2012-2013

. . . .

Being a part of Lunch Ladies changed me. It helped me learn to look at people as souls. It made me realize that when a visitor comes into church, we may be the only opportunity that person has to learn about Jesus and the Good News, so we need to reach out to those people, and those that we see struggling, every chance we get. It also helped me realize that we don't need to reach out to visitors alone, but we also need to make sure those inside the church are living their lives faithfully to God, and if they aren't, we need to help them in any way that we can because "everybody in the body matters to the body."

Looking back, the Lunch Ladies ministry taught me to be more evangelistic at school and in the community, taught me how to properly help those who were struggling, taught me how to be there for people when they needed it, and taught me how to be a better servant for the Lord.

—Brian, Lunch Lady 2012-2014

. . . .

Lunch Ladies was not just a meeting that I went to every Wednesday night before church. It wasn't just a chance for me to serve others and fill my quota for the week. It wasn't a chance for me to feel better about myself at all. Lunch Ladies wasn't about me; it wasn't about anyone in the room. Sure, it impacted each of us, some more than others, but Lunch Ladies was always about reaching out to the people around us for God.

It taught me to relentlessly pursue people for their souls' sake. And it continually reminded me of how much work we had to do and how important souls are. It was overwhelming at times, but we always had God and we always had each other.

It was such an amazing thing to be able to walk in to a room, afraid to talk to a visitor, and to know that you could go grab another Lunch Lady to tackle your fear with you, because it was worth it. A soul is worth it. It was encouraging to pause, look around the loud, crowded room and see other Lunch Ladies in action. They continually stepped up to the task and welcomed so many visitors. They were willing not to put the awkwardness aside, but to embrace it.

It was so exciting to come back to the next week's meeting and hear what God had done in just the past seven days! God doesn't get enough credit. We continually took time to encourage each other in the meetings, to look at what we were working with, to thank God for what He had blessed us with in the past week, and to thank God for allowing us to help in His ministry. It was such a privilege to be able to work with and be a part of the Lunch Ladies.

Being a part of the Lunch Ladies helped me get a better view into what ministry is all about. It helped me see that without strong leaders and people willing to take a chance for a greater cause, the church, our youth group, and God's Kingdom were not going to flourish. It simply helped me to see that it is not all about me. I learned a lot about the capacity that others have to serve even when you don't think they are necessarily gifted in a certain area. That is one of the wisest prerequisites to ministry that Philip taught me: you either have to have the gift for it or the heart for it; God can work with a willing heart.

—Emilie, Lunch Lady 2012-2014

PART 3
YOUR CAFETERIA

14

PREPARING THE SOIL

"YOU DID IT! CONGRATULATIONS!"

I want you to know that I've been praying for you to make it this far in the book.

Praying about the things that I am going to share with you. Praying that you will be inspired to take action. Praying about the potential ministries that could be launched across the nation for the Kingdom. Praying for souls to be reached. Praying for your leadership.

Praying for God to be glorified by all of our joint efforts.

I've seen God's power working through the Lunch Ladies ministry in amazing ways. I believe in this ministry, not because of what it is, but because Who's behind it.

I cannot wait to share Part Three of this book with you. Now, I want to walk you through the process of launching a Lunch Ladies ministry (or whatever name you choose for this ministry) wherever you are.

Maybe you've been trying to visualize what this ministry would look like in your congregation. There are probably a lot of questions and ideas swirling around in your head (I hope so because that means you're thinking about it seriously). Maybe you have even come up with a few reasons why this "won't work" where you are. Stay with me! I promise to do my best to address as many of those thoughts and ideas as I can in the coming chapters.

I want to begin this part of the book by sharing with you some principles about the important process of preparing the soil (the souls) for the launch of a Lunch Ladies ministry.

FARMER JOHN

It's interesting to think about John the Baptist's role in Jesus' ministry. John's job was to prepare the way for Jesus. He was a minister of preparation (maybe that's what you would find on his business card tucked inside the pocket of his camel hair blazer). He preached messages of repentance, declared that the Kingdom of Heaven was at hand, and baptized people who wanted to make changes in their lives.

Sound familiar? Jesus would go on to expound upon those three messages in greater and grander detail.

There are a lot of things God teaches us from the life of John, but one thing is this: The Lord knew the importance of "preparing the way" for ministry.

It fascinates me that God chose someone to prepare the way for Jesus. I mean this is Jesus we're talking about here. Did He really need someone to prepare the way for Him?

Jesus did a similar thing in Luke 10:1. "After this the Lord appointed seventy-two others and sent them on ahead of Him, two by two, into every town and place where He Himself was about to go."

Did Jesus need John? Did Jesus need the seventy-two?

The way I see it, if You can rise up from the dead, there's nothing You cannot do. I don't think Jesus needed anyone to fulfill His ministry for Him. But here's what we do know: Jesus saw value in preparing the soil.

God sent John to prepare the soil for Christ's ministry. Jesus sent the apostles to prepare the soil for His ministry. Likewise, you must prepare people for His ministry. And just as the farmer makes preparations for a great harvest, so must you prepare. That means you will need to labor hard--till the land, plant the seeds, weather the storms, and water the crops, all so that eventually, you can harvest fruit.

. . . .

HOW TO START A LUNCH LADIES MINISTRY

STEP #1: PRAY.

In keeping with the farmer analogy, it doesn't matter how great of a farmer you are, you cannot grow a seed. So it is with ministry. You do not have the ability to grow a seed.

It always makes me cringe whenever I hear ministers, elders, or anybody connected to a church talk about how much they grew the church.

No, **you** didn't have anything to do with that. "Neither he who plants nor he who waters is anything, but only God who gives the growth" (1 Corinthians 3:7).

God gives the increase, and the glory belongs to Him alone. And before you try taking it for yourself, you should know that the sentence for taking the glory away from God is death by worms (Acts 12:23).
It goes without saying (I hope) that you're going to need God to get this ministry off the ground. It also probably goes without saying that you are going to need to pray a lot. It doesn't matter how great you are--this ministry will thrive only if God is in it.

Psalm 127 is attributed to the wise king, Solomon, where it says,

> Unless the Lord builds the house,
> > those who build it labor in vain.
> Unless the Lord watches over the city,
> > the watchman stays awake in vain (Psalm 127:1).

Unless the Lord is the One building this ministry, you, too, are laboring and watching in vain.

Luke 6:12-13 lets us in on a little secret about what Jesus did before He began a great ministry with the twelve men that became the twelve apostles.

> In these days He went out to the mountain to pray, and all night He continued in prayer to God. And when day came, He called His disciples and chose from them twelve, whom He named apostles.

Jesus pulled an all-nighter in prayer on the day before He chose the twelve. I'd say that worked out pretty well.

You won't get very far into the book of Acts without seeing how significant prayer was to the first Christians. In the book of Acts alone, forms of the word *pray* (prays, prayed, prayer, praying, etc.) appear 30 times. They understood that without inquiring of the Lord, their plans were futile.

You can take your pick. You can take it from Solomon (the wisest man who ever lived), you can take it from the New Testament church (who saw the miraculous power of God at work), or you can take it from Jesus Himself (the miraculous power of God at work). When the Lord is in the process, people will be blessed.

So pray without ceasing (1 Thessalonians 5:17).

STEP #2: LET THE WORD SPEAK.

The story of the Lunch Ladies did not happen because of my vision. It did not happen because of my passion. Nobody was transformed because of me. Nobody was moved because of my strong desire for things to be better.

Neither will it be with you.

This story began where all great stories begin: the Word of God. It began in Acts 6 with the story of the widows being neglected, and God took over from there.

When the message comes from the Word of God, it makes **all** the difference. All Scripture is breathed out by God and profitable for teaching, for reproof, for correction, and for training in righteousness, that the man of God may be complete, equipped for every good work (2 Timothy 3:16-17).

The Word of God can do a whole lot more than I can. It comes with authority.

> For the word of God is living and powerful, and sharper than any two-edged sword, piercing even to the division of soul and spirit, and of joints and marrow, and is a discerner of the thoughts and intents of the heart. And there is no creature hidden from His sight, but all things are naked and open to the eyes of Him to whom we must give account (Hebrews 4:12-13, NKJV).

The Word can cut deeper than any sword because it can touch a place that no sword can reach: the soul. The Word of God brings about conviction that brings about transformation. "Now when they had heard this, they were cut to the heart and said to Peter and the rest of the apostles, 'Men and brothers, what shall we do?'" (Acts 2:37, NKJV).

They were cut to the heart. When? When they heard God's message delivered by Peter.

> As he journeyed he came near Damascus, and suddenly a light shone around him from heaven. Then he fell to the ground, and heard a voice saying to him, "Saul, Saul, why are you persecuting Me?" And he said, "Who are You, Lord?" Then the Lord said, "I am Jesus, whom you are persecuting. It is hard for you to kick against the goads." So he, trembling and astonished, said, "Lord, what do You want me to do?"

(Acts 9:3-6a, NKJV).

Paul felt convicted to action when? When the Lord spoke to him. "And they said to one another, 'Did not our heart burn within us while He talked with us on the road, and while He opened the Scriptures to us?'" (Luke 24:32, NKJV). When Jesus met the two men on the road to Emmaus, when did their hearts burn? When Christ spoke to them—when the Word of God spoke to them.

The bad news is that it doesn't matter how badly you want to change things. You simply do not have that kind of power. The good news is that God does, and His Word changes things. Literally. Things change at His Word.

And so let the Word speak and let It do what only It can do.

You will need to deliver powerful messages from God's Word about reaching souls. It might be with a stand-alone class like Esmin Green (you're welcome to use the notes from my "Esmin Green" lesson if you think they would help), it might be a series, or it might be something totally different like a special activity. But regardless of what you choose, **you must allow the Word of God to do what it does best: change hearts**.

If people are convicted and convinced that something is God's will, they will do it.

I have no authority. He does.

I cannot change people. He does.

I cannot change cultures. He does.

15

RECRUITING

SO YOU WANNA LAUNCH A LUNCH LADIES MINISTRY?

Here's a checklist of what we've covered so far:

1. You've prepared the soil prayerfully.

2. You've prepared the soil with a message (or messages) like "Esmin Green," allowing the Word of God to speak to the hearts of your group, convicting them of the need for relevant, relentless, soul-seeking ministry.

THE SECRET SERVICE

Last week I received an email from David who shared with me a little bit about a Lunch Ladies ministry that his group started back in the beginning of this year called "The Secret Service."

> I had a group of about 8 that met with me every week throughout the spring. This group reached out to several kids (you know the type--kids who were not very involved). They started sitting with them during services (if they wouldn't come sit with the youth group). They really made a difference in one of our 11th graders who started getting more involved and stepped out of his comfort zone and went on a mission trip with us back in the summer. The Secret Service group cooled off during the summer and a couple have asked me to start it back up again. I got a little discouraged because I started the whole process by talking about those who are neglected (and showed

> the Esmin Green video), and out of fifty teens, I had eight to come to the first meeting.

There were a lot of great parts to David's email but the part that jumped out at me the most was the part where he opened up about being discouraged (maybe I'm a pessimist for zeroing in on that aspect). I know that David is not alone in his discouragement. In fact, there are probably some of you realists that have already anticipated a similar fate for your Lunch Ladies ministry.

If you've ever attempted to dream something up, you know how much it stings to have a harsh reality like this come your way.

"What went wrong? I prayed! The message was right! What happened?"

. . . .

THE PROCESS

You probably know who Nick Saban is. Saban is the football coach at the University of Alabama. Love him or hate him, he has been extremely successful, winning 4 B.C.S. National Championships at the time of this writing. He is one of only two coaches to win titles under two different teams. He also won B.C.S. National Championship Games three times within a four-year span. It seems that each year he has his team in a position to make another national title run.

How does he do it?

Well, if you could completely answer that question, you'd have millions of dollars, and you'd probably be the next coach in line to succeed him at the Capstone. I'm not sure anybody fully knows the answer, but one thing's for sure: Saban understands the importance of recruiting in building a team.

At the time of this writing in 2015, Saban has once again landed the nation's number one ranked recruiting class, just as he has every year since his arrival in 2007. He recruits potential, builds a team, and celebrates a lot of victories.

Godly leadership understands the significance behind those three principles as well: We must look to recruit those who have hearts for ministry, we must develop a team, and we must celebrate God's victories.

. . . .

THIS AIN'T TEEBALL

Early on in ministry, I made the mistake of believing that everybody belonged on a team.

I probably would've vehemently argued with you if you tried to convince me otherwise. I probably would've been super-offended if you disagreed with me. I probably would've thought you were an ungodly idiot. I probably would've used a lot of Bible verses to back up my viewpoint.

But there is nothing "probably" about this: I was an idiot.

A few years, and a bunch of mistakes (and headaches) later, I have come to an understanding of a hard truth: not everybody belongs on a team.

Christianity isn't teeball--not everybody gets a trophy (1 Corinthians 9:24).

Not everybody who says, "Lord, Lord" will enter the Kingdom of Heaven (Matthew 7:21).

Not everybody gets to be an elder (1 Timothy 3:1-7).

Not everybody needs to be a teacher (James 3:1).

Not everybody got to be an apostle--Jesus chose 12 not 12 trillion. Jesus didn't say, "Hey, you wanna be My disciple?!? You do?!? Great! Then you're in!"

No.

In fact, there were some that Christ Himself deemed "unworthy" of being called "His." "He who loves father or mother more than Me is not worthy of Me. And he who loves son or daughter more than Me is not worthy of Me. And he who does not take his cross and follow after Me is not worthy of Me" (Matthew 10:37-38). My 20-year-old self would hate me for saying this, but some people are not fit to lead (or even follow, according to Jesus).

To put it simply, some people are great candidates for a Lunch Ladies ministry and some are not.

So, how do you sort through who is and who isn't a great candidate for Lunch Ladies? Unless you've got a "sorting hat" (and if you have a sorting hat, where did you get one?!? I have to know this!!!), it can be sort of a tricky process. The beauty in what I'm about to share with you is that you aren't the one who ultimately decides. Following this process in recruiting a team will solve you a lot of headaches.

Here's how to do it.

. . . .

STEP #1: SET A DATE FOR THE FIRST MEETING AND STRIKE WHILE THE IRON'S HOT.

Make plans to hold your first Lunch Ladies meeting the week after your "Esmin Green" message. This will ensure that you build momentum at the right time.

STEP #2: EXTEND AN INVITATION.

Matthew 22 is one of my favorite parables of Jesus. In it we read of a king who is planning to host a great wedding feast for his son, and the story picks up with the king working on the guest list.

The story paints a beautiful, almost heartbreaking picture of a king's desperate invitation. The loving king, longing to share with others the joy that his son has brought to him, invites as many people as he can find. Many are called, but few choose to attend.

Obviously, this parable was not written about Lunch Ladies, but the point I want to make here is that God has invited us all to be a part of something special. I recommend doing the same.

You could extend this invitation via text, Facebook, bulletin, or run-of-the-mill announcement. I recommend sending a mass text to your high school students, a day or two removed from your Esmin Green message, advertising a meeting (I did this after our transformative CYC weekend in Gatlinburg). Here's an example of what that message might look like if you were to send it out via text message.

> Hey, guys! Really, really enjoyed the message last night about Esmin Green. I appreciate all of the things that were said and the desire that so many of you have to make things better. Next week on Wednesday night at 6:00 in room 202 we are going to have a meeting for any of you guys that have been baptized that would like to continue the conversation about reaching out to people like Esmin Green. Hope to see you there!

That simple text accomplishes two important things. One, it catches the attention of the spiritually serious, and two, it prevents people from being able to say that you play favorites.

And by the way, don't play favorites. God shows no partiality; neither should we. You are God's favorite. Do ministry in such a way that would prove time and time again that all of the students are your favorites. Mini-rant over. Remember, **everybody** gets invited (Matthew 22).

STEP #3: MAKE A LIST.

Don't rely on a massive invitation (text, email) to get the recruiting job done. You will need to figure out who needs to be at your first Lunch Ladies meeting for it to be a success. There are many people in the congregation (or students in the youth group) that already do a great job reaching out to souls--the thing that you are getting ready to emphasize. Bring those people into that meeting. It will be natural for them to be there.

I recommend a ratio of 1 Lunch Lady per every 5 people actively involved in your youth program. (So a youth group with 100 students in it would need around 20 Lunch Ladies.) If you have too few Lunch Ladies, the group will probably be overwhelmed. If you have too many Lunch Ladies, the group will probably feel like they aren't contributing and will probably stop showing up for meetings. The 1:5 ratio Lunch Lady to member should help make sure there is plenty of work to go around.

If you are planning to set up this kind of ministry on a congregational level, the model changes slightly. Can you imagine how long meetings would be if you had 100 Lunch Ladies talking about the 500 people in your congregation they were reaching out to?

At Mt. Juliet church of Christ, every Sunday morning adult Bible class has a version of Lunch Ladies that we call our "All For One" ministry that was actually built upon the Lunch Ladies model.

It's called "All for One" because to the shepherd, the chance to save one sheep was enough to leave behind 99 others. To the woman, finding one lost coin was worth pulling an all-nighter with a lamp and a broom in hand tearing an entire house apart. To the father, the one rebellious son's return was worth a ring, a robe, a feast, and a celebration.

The Good Shepherd, the diligent woman, and the loving Father did it all for one. If we want to be compassionate, courageous, and caring like the Good Shepherd, if we want to be diligent, relentless workers like the woman, if we want to be welcoming, forgiving, and loving like our heavenly Father, we, too, must be "all for one."

Our All For One groups meet every two weeks and get together to celebrate, update, invest, and pray. They zero in on reaching people that are natural fits for their demographic. For example, if a young married couple moved into the area and visited Mt. Juliet, it would be natural for our Sunday morning Bible class loaded with young married couples to be the class to follow up and reach out to them.

Also of note, due to our congregation's shepherding model, every adult Bible class has an elder in it who is closely connected to the members inside of that room. It sounds like a small detail, but it has paid big dividends having our shepherds more closely connected to the flock. It has helped our membership and eldership build a relationship.

Finally, every adult Bible class also has a class coordinator. One of the roles of the class coordinator is to be in charge of "running the meeting." So it is important for this person to have a good grasp of what the purpose of the All For One ministry is.

Chances are, you fall into one of these categories:

1. The youth ministry/congregation where you attend is small, or the youth ministry/ congregation where you attend is large.

2. You've got a few people in mind that you believe would be a perfect fit for this ministry, or you can't think of single person in your youth program/congregation that would be a good fit in this ministry.

3. The students/congregation where you attend would never go for this, or the students/congregation where you attend would be all over this.

4. You think: "This could work: My students/congregation need(s) this!" or you think "This will not work. My students/congregation do/does not need this."

5. You can't imagine 3 people showing up to a meeting on a Wednesday night at 6:00, or you can totally imagine having 30 people show up to a meeting on a Wednesday night, so long as you serve steaks and take them to Disney World afterwards.

Regardless of where you are on that scale, you can make this ministry work. I've been in meetings where there were only 3 people in the room, but all 3 came because they were serious about reaching out to and caring for souls. Any time you spend talking about caring for souls is time well spent!

If you still have questions about how this ministry would look and work where you are, I'm thankful because it means you're thinking about carrying out these concepts in the real world. Later on in the book, we will spend more time discussing what this ministry might look like where you are, be it in a church of 1,000 or in a classroom of 5.

But for now let's turn our attention back to the list of recruits. Again, this isn't a list of your favorite people. This is a strategic list.

A contractor wouldn't hire just anyone to do construction. You wouldn't ask a random stranger off the street to perform your open-heart surgery.

So it goes with Lunch Ladies: the people that you recruit to be in Lunch Ladies need to be the right kind of people.

When I first started recruiting students for Lunch Ladies, I made a list of people that I wanted to recruit based on four criteria.

1. Is this person a Christian?

2. Does this person possess a natural ability for reaching out to people?

3. What group of people could this person potentially reach?

4. Does this person have a willing heart to reach out to people?

While there were some good reasons and thoughts behind those four criteria, I now only use numbers one (Is this person a Christian?) and four (Does this person have a willing heart to reach out to people?) in recruiting Lunch Ladies.

I mean think about it: a Christian with a willing heart to reach people? Who cares whether or not it's his or her "natural talent"? **God will take a Christian with a willing heart every time.**

I would have never guessed that some of our greatest leaders would become some of our greatest leaders.

One of the coolest things in this ministry has been watching students become something else by the power of Christ working in them. There have been some really, really quiet kids in Lunch Ladies. How in the world could quiet kids be good at getting up out of their seats and going to talk to a complete stranger? It didn't come naturally to them. It was the Spirit of God, the supernatural, at work within them (Ephesians 3:20). Their determination to make things better and to follow God's will pushed them beyond their comfort zone.

And who cares whether or not she's friends with this girl or that guy who could potentially reach this girl or that guy (#3 on my old list of criteria)? God's plan is to use Christians willing to reach whomever however!

STEP #4: MAKE A INTENTIONALLY VAGUE PHONE CALL ABOUT THE MEETING.

So, now that you've issued an invitation to come to a meeting that's happening within the next week, and now that you've got a list of people that you know you want to be in Lunch Ladies, it's time to make some phone calls.

If your meeting is happening on a Wednesday night (like our Lunch Ladies meetings do), I recommend calling people on Monday. Sunday is too far removed (they'll forget), Tuesday is kind of short notice, and if your phone call about a "really important meeting" is happening the same day as this "really important meeting," you've sort of shown that it's not a "really important meeting."

So call on Monday (or, use the same reasoning if your meeting is happening on a Sunday).

Now it's time to make a phone call to tell them all about the ministry that you know all about but they've never heard of and know nothing about!

Sound like fun?

If that sounds overwhelming, don't worry. You're not telling them about Lunch Ladies yet, so don't get ahead of yourself! All you have to do up to this point is call them and get them to come to a meeting.

Here's an example of how my "recruiting" phone calls typically go. (You saw an example of this kind of phone call in Chapter 6.)

"Hey, man! It's Philip! What's up?"

"Oh, nothing much, man. Just hanging out at home."

"Awesome. You doing ok?"

(More small talk, until finally...)

"Hey, I know this is random, but did you get my text earlier, like last week, about the meeting we're going to have Wednesday night before church about the Esmin Green stuff?"

"Oh, yeah. I remember seeing that."

"Ok, good. I was hoping my text went through! Anyway, I wanted to call you because that meeting is going to be really, really important. We're going to be talking about some things that are going to be huge for the youth group. And I know that's a little hazy, but I will tell you more once we get there. I really need you there. We are meeting at 6:00 in room 100. Do you think there's any way you can make it?"

Sometimes I even leave the details of the meeting hazier than I did in that example. The phone call needs to be interesting enough to pique people's curiosity. And unless they've got something crazy going on that they cannot get out of, that's all it takes to get them to the meeting. They're in.

Two quick points here before we move on to Step #5.

On some rare occasions you'll recruit someone for the Lunch Ladies kickoff meeting that won't show. If you recruit someone but they don't show up for the meeting, I suggest leaving it alone. Let them bring it up if they choose to. If they bring it up and they're apologetic about it and they offer up a reason for missing the meeting that sounds legit, I would fill them in and explain what you did at the meeting. On the other hand, sometimes you'll have someone show up at a Lunch Ladies kickoff meeting that you didn't recruit by phone call. Earlier I mentioned how you aren't the one that ultimately decides how all of the Lunch Ladies team-building process pans out. Perhaps a recruit not showing up is God's way of answering your prayers. Maybe that person that you thought was the perfect fit for this ministry isn't the right fit right now. That's not the end of the world. It doesn't make them any less important than anyone else. Remember, this isn't a ministry for "your favorites." It's a ministry opportunity for Christians interested in this kind of opportunity.

And as for that person who showed up to the meeting that you didn't expect: that's just gravy! Perhaps it is also God's will to involve them. If they got a text from you that advertised an important meeting about reaching souls five or six days before the actual meeting and they showed up, that tells you something about the kind of heart they have!

STEP #5: PREPARE A COVENANT FOR THE MEETING.

What I'm about to share with you is something that I wish I had thought through from the very first time the Lunch Ladies had ever met.

Imagine you invited a high school student to come to the first Lunch Ladies meeting. At the time you asked them, they were on spiritually on fire. They were as strong as they could be, and as Lunch Ladies continued, you continued to lean on that student heavily to get things done, and lead mightily in the youth program.

But then the fire began to dwindle (as most fires do at some point), and suddenly this spiritual leader is struggling in a big way, making some bad decisions, and everybody knows it. Yet, all the while they're still coming to Lunch Ladies, trying to lead, pretending like everything is okay when in reality, nothing could be further from the truth.

Truthfully, that's probably been any of us at some point in our lives. Hypocrisy, immaturity, complacency, apathy, burnout—-we know them all too well.

Looking back, I probably recruited some people to be in Lunch Ladies that weren't spiritually ready. I'm not saying they were bad people, but perhaps they weren't ready to be in a position of leadership at the time I asked them to be. Others needed to be able to feel like they could step out of Lunch Ladies to avoid burnout or to get things back where they needed to be.

It took nearly a year and a half of stuff like that happening to figure out that we needed a Lunch Ladies Covenant. Below is a copy of what ours looks like. Obviously, you can create a covenant that communicates, emphasizes, and accomplishes what you want.

. . . .

THE LUNCH LADIES COVENANT

Then He said to His disciples, "The harvest is plentiful, but the laborers are few; therefore pray earnestly to the Lord of the harvest to send out laborers into His harvest" (Matthew 9:37-38).

I. 6:15 meetings every Wednesday...**Be there**!

II. No gossip! This is not a time to get out all the things you hate about people or how much this person annoys you. We are here to talk about how to help the hurt.

III. Reach in––hold yourself accountable! You cannot lead someone to something you are not following yourself!

IV. Reach out––no one goes unspoken to! It's our job to not only make people feel welcome but also included. Remember, we're Lunch Ladies: Love all. Serve all.

V. Follow through––the assignments you take and are given are serious. So follow through with them! This isn't about saying how many people you talked to or about checking someone's name off of a list. This is about making relationships for God!

VI. Bring something to the table. Listen, we're all hungry here, and if you don't bring something to the table, we don't eat. It's that simple. So speak up in meetings! If you're not sharing your thoughts then we don't know what's going on in the kingdom. **You** were asked to be in this group for a reason, so speak up.

VII. Either you're in or you're out. Seriously! This is a group that demands you step up and step out of your comfort zone. Get really comfortable with being really uncomfortable. If you can't handle that, then this isn't the group for you.

I will uphold the Lunch Ladies Covenant to the best of my ability.

Signed: _____

. . . .

Now at every "kickoff" (the first meeting of the new school year; we take a break in the summer) Lunch Ladies meeting, we put a copy of The Lunch Ladies Covenant in the hands of every student. We talk about how important that this ministry is, go over every item on the covenant, and let them know that this is what we expect of one another.

We don't want them to rush into making an important decision too quickly one way or the other, so we tell them to take a week to think it over and pray about it. We ask our students to bring back a signed covenant to the next Lunch Ladies meeting if they'd like to be involved in this ministry.

I also let them know that if they don't feel like they can uphold the covenant, it's okay not to be part of it! I promise them there will be no hard feelings on my part, and that I won't be mad at them or treat them any differently if they decide not to be a Lunch Lady. After all, I've asked them to carefully, prayerfully consider this decision. How foolish would it be for me as a leader to be upset if their answer is "No"?

. . . .

DAMAGE CONTROL

I had no idea who Chris and Daniel were but it didn't take long for them to impress me. As it turned out, they were a couple of senior boys from another large youth group in Nashville, and they had come on a mission. They came not to gripe, or to badmouth their youth minister or youth program, or to cast stones, but they, too, were frustrated with a trend that they saw within their youth group.

And while they were describing the way things were, I couldn't help but think how familiar their frustrations felt.

And so they came, not to gossip, but to address some things that they saw as issues standing between the way things were and the way things needed to be. They were hungry for ideas.

I shared with them the story of the Lunch Ladies and a few of the ways that God has used it to address some of our issues at Mt. Juliet. Over the next few weeks, we kept the conversation going while I tried my best to support these two guys who had a great desire to see God's will be done.

They had the right motivation, the right idea, and their hearts were in the right place, but the model was never adopted. When I asked them what happened, they mentioned that "one of the bigger challenges was finding people that were willing to be a part of the group because it was a secretive thing, and they thought it may do more damage than not."

Looking back, I wish I hadn't made such a big deal about the secret aspect of this ministry. What's truly the most important thing is that Christians who are interested in living out this ministry are made aware of it. If you're a Christian, God's invited you to be a part of His mission. His invitation is all that we need! So jump in!

You've put in some serious work. Many prayers have been prayed, the Word has been implanted, and now the team is coming together. Get ready for the new highlight of your week...

16

MEETING EXPECTATIONS

SO YOU WANNA LAUNCH A LUNCH LADIES MINISTRY?

Here's a checklist of what we've covered so far:

1. You've prepared the soil prayerfully.

2. You've prepared the soil with a message (or messages) like "Esmin Green," allowing the Word of God to speak to the hearts of your group, convicting them of the need for relevant, relentless, soul-seeking ministry.

3. You've set up a meeting after the week of your "Esmin Green" message.

4. You've prepared a covenant, a list of expectations that the group has for themselves.

5. You've advertised the meeting by sending out an invitation to all Christians who might have a willing heart to be involved in this ministry.

6. You've also called some individuals that you believe may play a big role in this ministry and pushed hard to get them there. At the same time, remember, you're not closing the door of opportunity for this ministry on any willing Christian! If someone shows up that you didn't consider, that reveals something about the kind of heart he or she has!

THE INTERVIEW

All eyes were on me. To say that I was nervous is an understatement. I was sitting inside a room full of people, and I was interviewing to become part of my college's University Program Council. It was a huge deal to me. A lot of my campus heroes were part of that group--people with loads of creativity, great personalities, and great senses of humor.

It was the sought-after second interview, and so far it was going well. Until...

"If you could be a character in any movie, who would you be and why?"

I panicked a bit. Superman was the first thing that came to mind, but I was sure it was the first thing that came to every other guy's mind, too, so there was no way I was going to say Superman. Besides, think of all the creativity inside the room. Superman was the safe answer, the cliché of clichés. No way I was going with Superman on this one.

"Hmmmm..." I said, "I guess...I'll have to go with..."

What movies had I seen? Why couldn't I think of a single cool character from a movie? Anybody but Superman. What had movies had I seen lately?

And that's the only explanation I can offer for what came out of my mouth next: "I guess...I would be the guy who stopped *The Passion of the Christ*, because, man, I know he's not actually a character, but man, that was heavy..."

Was this actually my answer? Was I really saying this?

I actually remember looking around the room and seeing the expression on everybody's face. It was as if they were watching a train wreck in slow motion.

"Actually, you know what? Can we do that again? Ask me again, because I was also thinking Superman."

Needless to say, I didn't get into the University Program Council. Also I'm thankful that I didn't stop the Passion of the Christ.

If you don't have any idea what to say in the first Lunch Ladies meeting, there's no need to panic. I won't set you up for an epic fail. In fact, the content of our very first Lunch Ladies meeting is here for you, word for word, in Chapter 6 (see "The Lunch Ladies Launch"). Copy, add, or remove anything from the notes that you believe would benefit your ministry.

. . . .

STARTING RIGHT

However you choose to say it, know that this first meeting has to especially be done right. It must communicate clearly the vision and purpose of this ministry, as well as inspire willing hearts to take action. Be prayerful, know that God will be with you, and remember what can happen when even one Christian has the conviction and the courage to step out in faith (see Chapter 10)!

Get ready for the new highlight of your week every week: regular Lunch Ladies meetings.

Regular meetings? Wait a minute, how regular are we talking? People hate meetings. Nobody will show up to these week in and week out.

People don't hate meetings. People hate "waste-of-my-time" meetings where nothing significant takes place and nothing gets done. That's just it: meetings when a lot of significant things take place and a lot of things get done are meetings we love. Those meetings are the meetings for which meetings were invented!

People don't hate Lunch Ladies meetings. They've never been to one (so how could they?), and I can guarantee you one thing: You run these meetings effectively and it will never feel like a waste of time.

Yes, regular meetings are important, but what's even more important is the way you run the meeting. What I'm about to say to you is very blunt, but I'm not sure I can emphasize it enough: Your influence will either bless or curse this ministry.

Back in Chapter 14, I talked a lot about how God is the only one with the power to change hearts and the only one who can give the increase.

This is also true: While you **cannot** grow the seed, you **can** cultivate the soil.

In fact, you must. If a leader does not set the tone for the culture of this ministry, something or someone else will.

Want proof? How about the entire book of Judges?

Judges 17:6 and 21:25 say the exact same thing: "In those days there was no king in Israel. Everyone did what was right in his own eyes" (NKJV).

And so we read story after story about what happens when a strong leader does not hold God's people to a higher standard, and it isn't pretty. The Israelites were never great followers, but they always did better when they had a strong leader (like Moses, Joshua, David, etc.) who was determined to uphold God's plan for the culture.

The leadership must be determined to lead, set the tone, and cultivate the soil so that seeds can be nurtured and God can give the increase.

Needless to say, the way that you lead these meetings is absolutely critical. I want to share with you some of the lessons that I have learned (some of them the hard way) about what does and does not work in leading Lunch Ladies meetings. The Lord has allowed me to be a part of some great wins, and the Lord has also allowed me to be a part of some losses. I hope you'll follow my advice here. I'm not trying to "throw my weight around" or come across like I know everything there is to know about ministry (I don't!), but I do know a lot of things that do and do not work in regards to this one.

LUNCH LADIES MEETING EXPECTATION #1
MEET IN PERSON, MEET REGULARLY, AND MEET IN THE SAME LOCATION.

Let me put this to you plain and simple: you cannot do this ministry effectively without regularly scheduled face-to-face meetings.

Emails will not get it done. A Facebook group will not get it done. Group texts won't get it done. Skype or Google Hangouts won't get it done. Meeting once a month won't get it done.

There is no replacement for a face-to-face meeting. Period.

Want proof? Talk to an Army wife and see if she'd rather talk to her husband via Skype or face to face. Technology is great, but it cannot replace the energy inside of a room filled with real, live people.

In my own personal experience, I have learned that I cannot do Lunch Ladies effectively without meeting every week.

I promise you, if you miss a week, you're going to get behind. Something will go undone. Someone will drop a ball. A guest will go unnoticed. A time-sensitive opportunity will slip away. Group morale will dwindle, and you'll begin to feel disconnected from one another. Your list of people to reach will be twice as long. Trust me you won't have time to get to everything you need to get to within a half-hour slot, and in the three years that I've been running these meetings, I don't think we have ever gotten done early!

Can you meet every other week instead of every week? I know that our All For One ministries (Lunch Ladies on a congregational level) do at Mt. Juliet, but I only know what has worked for us, and meeting every other week isn't what has worked for us. If it came down to meeting every other week versus never meeting at all, I'd chose meeting every other week! Any meeting would be better than none at all!

I would also add that people can remember regularly scheduled meetings better, so they're not left wondering week after week, "Hey, do we meet this Wednesday, or is that in two more weeks? Oh, and what time? Oh, and where do we meet again?"

LUNCH LADIES MEETING EXPECTATION #2
DO NOT BROADCAST MEETINGS.

We don't advertise our weekly meetings to the general public. Remember, initially, the general public was invited (via a mass text, announcement, etc.). They chose not to come, and so you are simply meeting with the people who did decide to come.

I have always operated this ministry under the idea that all it would take is one disgruntled person to do some significant damage. Some bitter soul looking to stir up some drama would figure out a way to put a spin on this ministry that is false.

"Well, you know Philip's favorites in the youth group get together every week for a secret meeting and talk about people, right?"

And there you go. Damage done. Cue up the rumor mill. Get ready for a sit-down with your elders and a family (or families).

Obviously, you need to communicate with the Lunch Ladies about meeting times, but leave the general public out of it. I send out a text to the Lunch Ladies every week reminding them of our Wednesday night meetings. The Lunch Ladies ministry has operated well flying under the radar, and behind the scenes, and "If it ain't broke..."

LUNCH LADIES MEETING EXPECTATION #3
CELEBRATE.

These are the four major parts to every Lunch Ladies meeting.

1. Celebrate.
2. Update.
3. Invest.
4. Pray.

(And if I had to include a #5, it would be "Cheer." Remember the "We feel awkward so you don't have to!" cheer?)

The first aspect of the meeting is "celebration." I hope that the concept of celebrating is not one that is lost on us in the church. In fact, celebration shouldn't be confined into the quarters of a meeting. Celebration, closely related to words like *praise*, *worship*, and *thanksgiving*, ought to be an every day aspect of a Christian's life.
Heaven celebrates when a sinner comes home (Luke 15:7). The Father celebrated when His dead child came home alive (Luke 15:20-24). Paul wrote to the Christians in Philippi, "Rejoice in the Lord always. Again I will say, rejoice!" (Philippians 4:4), and to the Christians in Thessalonica "...in everything give thanks; for this is the will of God in Christ Jesus for you" (1 Thessalonians 5:18). Psalm 77:11-14 says, "I will remember the works of the Lord; Surely I will remember Your wonders of old. I will also meditate on all Your work, And talk of Your deeds. Your way, O God, is in the sanctuary; Who is so great a God as our God? You are the God who does wonders; You have declared Your strength among the peoples" (NKJV).

The first thing I do every week in our Lunch Ladies meeting is write the word *celebrate* on our white board and open up the floor by saying, "Ok, let's take a moment to think about what we have seen God doing this past week. What are some things worth celebrating this week?"

I always walk into the room with a couple of things in mind to get the ball rolling just in case the room falls silent (that happens occasionally). After you mention something worth celebrating, it'll usually refresh their minds. Open the floor back up, give them a chance to respond, and jot down the other "celebration" items that they mention.

I want you to imagine doing this exercise in the congregation where you attend. If you asked your congregation (or your Bible class, or high schoolers', or the eldership, or a ladies' class, or your senior group, etc.) that question, what are some things that they would list as things worth celebrating?

Here are a few ideas of some things that we might have written on our whiteboard any given week:

"Last week, Josh got baptized!"

"Jenna came to devo for the first time ever."

"We finally got Carson to sit with the youth group on Sunday night instead of with his parents."

"I saw Andrew get up out of his seat to go and sit and talk to Nathan, that kid who always sits by himself."

"Stephanie said she's going to come on the retreat next weekend!"

"I got a text from Abbie saying that she'll be here tonight!"

"Alex talked to me!"

"I had a really great conversation with Lindsey about church. She came last week for the first time and she said she really, really likes it here."

"I had a Bible study with Joe this past week."

"Brian brought a friend for the first time!"

"We had 6 guests this past week."

"We set a new record for our fall retreat!"

"I've noticed that Laura and Taylor are starting to hang out, which is really cool, because neither of them had someone that they really seemed to 'click' with in the youth group."

"Tiffany came back to church. We haven't seen her here in a year."

Stuff like that.

Week in and week out, you need to celebrate what God is doing, giving Him the glory, and you need to celebrate the individuals in the Lunch Ladies that are doing what the ministry is designed to do! Publicly and privately pour encouragement into them and reinforce the good habits that you see forming in the group. If you see Rebecca introducing herself to a first-time guest brag on her in front of the group. If you hear that Tyler and John invited Brandon to go out to eat with the youth group, mention that in front of the group. If the Lunch Ladies "owned" the entire room last week before class and they met all kinds of guests and nobody went unnoticed, make a big a deal about it.

When you see them doing instead of just talking about doing, it's beautiful; so let them know how beautiful it is to watch them work. Taking the time to recognize those who are doing what the ministry is designed to do will reinforce the mission and give the ones in the room a little boost from their leader.

This line stuck with me from DeVries' book *Sustainable Youth Ministry*.

> *Almost every time Adam met with the ESquad, he told a tale of one of its members going above and beyond. As the 'bard' of the ESquad, Adam's stories shaped the identity of the group, reminding them that they were the ones who were successfully taking away the awkward edge for a self-conscious newcomer (or for an old-timer who hasn't yet found his or her niche).*[5]

Obviously, celebrating is important, because the Bible says it is, but there's another reason why celebrating is **huge** when it comes to this

---

[5] *Sustainable Youth Ministry* by Mark DeVries. "The Magnet Effect" p.170.

ministry. If you don't take the time to acknowledge the hand of God at work in this ministry, it will feel like nothing good is ever happening. And spoiler alert: something good is always happening. So take time to celebrate––to define a win, to acknowledge progress, and to show the team that what they are doing is making a difference.

Remember the ingredients to a boring meeting?

LUNCH LADIES MEETING EXPECTATION #4
UPDATE.

Now comes the part where you go around the room and everybody gives a quick update on who they were supposed to be reaching out to the week before.

It's very important for everybody in the room to speak up.

I think sometimes that some of the best comments in the room are the ones we never get to hear. Whenever you open up the floor for discussion there are always "the usual suspects," those who are quick and willing to voice their opinion (whether you like it or not!). Unless there is a format in which everyone is required to speak, you won't get to hear from those who are more reserved, and many times it's the quieter, more cautious individuals that have better comments––they've been sitting there carefully thinking through what you're asking them to think through! The old adage is often true: "Still waters run deep."

The "Update" portion of the meeting might look something like this:

"Alright, Lauren, whatcha got for us?"

"I was supposed to reach out to Heather this past week, so I texted her and she said she was coming back again tonight!"

"Hey, that's great news, Lauren! Great job! Anything else?"

"No. That's all I've got this week," she says.

"Hey, thanks for doing that! Nice work! Alright, Craig, whatcha got for us tonight?

Craig's list (see what I did there?) wasn't as fruitful as Lauren's.

"Well, I had Jonathan, and I texted him to see if he wanted to come to the movies with a few of the guys from church Friday night but he never responded."

Instead of talking about how big of a jerk Jonathan is, and polling the room to see what they all think of him, instead turn your attention back to the one who did all he could do to reach him. "Hey, it's ok! You did your part, man! You can't make people respond to a text, but hey, you gave him an opportunity. Thanks for making an effort! Awesome."

Another great byproduct of the "going around the room" approach is what takes place when someone doesn't do his job: accountability.

"Alright, Mike, got anything for us tonight?"

"Well, ummmmm, I was supposed to talk to Justin...but I forgot."

A group of teenagers responds to this with a healthy heaping of positive peer pressure--they relish in heckling, joking, and taking advantage of the opportunity to tell him how terrible of a person that he is. They give them a hard time (the person who didn't do his part always takes it well), and it's usually pretty funny, but it sends a message: we expect each other to do his part (see items V and VI in "The Lunch Ladies Covenant").

LUNCH LADIES MEETING EXPECTATION #5
INVEST.

The third major aspect of every Lunch Ladies meeting is the part that we call "Invest." It's where everybody in the room leaves with a name of an individual that they are going to reach out to over the course of the next week. Sometimes I will enter a meeting with a list of names prepared that I want us to invest in, ranging anywhere from 20 to 80 names, and other times we let them generate the list of names themselves. We put the list up on the board and everybody takes names off the list.

We used to call the "Invest" portion of the meeting "Assign," but a few years ago a man by the name of Jaime Harper said something that stuck with me (I have crazy A.D.D. so if something sticks with me longer than 5 or 10 minutes, there's usually something to it), and changed the way that I thought about this approach. Jaime has spent the last several years of his life investing in people, ministering to their needs, teaching them to fight against Satan, and speaking into their hearts the love and the Truth of God.

> "Imagine that I had a bunch of empty water bottles sitting up all over the floor in this room, and I also had a huge bucket of water. If I asked you to fill up all the water bottles in this room, what would be the best way to do that? I could take that bucket and fling out the water all over the room, and yeah, there might be a little bit of water in some of the bottles, but you know what the best way to fill those bottles would be? To take the bucket over to one and to pour into it, and fill it, and then, after that one was full, move to the next bottle, pour into it, and fill it, and then the next bottle, and the next bottle, and so on."

We used to give our Lunch Ladies assignments. But people are not assignments (and when people become assignments, we lose sight of what true ministry is).

Now instead of making assignments, we ask our Lunch Ladies to make investments: To whom are you going to "pour" your time, your heart, and your energy into over the course of the next week?

When you think of things that way, ministry becomes more than just "shooting someone a text message." It becomes about doing whatever it takes to reach them!

Paul understood that winning souls for the Lord required him to use different techniques and approaches.

> For though I am free from all men, I have made myself a servant to all, that I might win the more; and to the Jews I became as a Jew, that I might win Jews; to those who are under the law, as under the law, that I might win those who are under the law; to those who are without law, as without law (not being without law toward God, but under law toward Christ, that I might win those who are without law; to the weak I became as weak, that I might win the weak. I have become all things to all men, that I might by all means save some. Now this I do for the Gospel's sake, that I may be partaker of it with you. (1 Corinthians 9:19-23, NKJV).

Every Lunch Lady leaves the room with at least one person's name in whom they will spend some time investing. We also have a rule that nobody takes more than three people's names. It's sort of like that water bottle analogy: investments take time. You can't make quality investments into individuals with a shotgun style approach. You have to pour into an individual, filling them with love, and again, that takes time.

Keep in mind the underlying purpose of this entire ministry is to reach out to people in whatever way we can. There is a lot to consider here when it comes to investing in people.

. . . .

NATURAL SELECTION

One of the reasons why it works so well to have the Lunch Ladies choose the individuals that they will invest in is because they usually feel connected to the person that they are reaching out to in some way. It usually isn't awkward for them to say something to the person that they select, because they already have some sort of relationship with him.

If the person is a guest, it would make the most sense for a Lunch Lady who met him or knows him to follow up with him. Maybe the guest was in the Lunch Lady's Cocoon (small group) on Wednesday night, maybe the guest is a Lunch Lady's neighbor, or a family friend, or someone that is in the same study hall.

If the person isn't a guest, but is someone that is in need of ministry, a Lunch Lady that has a good relationship with him needs to be the one reaching out to him.

. . . .

THE NEXT STEP

So you've got the name of an individual to whom you need to reach out. Now what?

Something we strongly emphasize when it comes to investing is sending the right message to the individuals that we are trying to reach.

You wouldn't send a "Get Well Soon" card to someone who lost their grandfather, or a sympathy card with a wedding gift (unless you have a twisted sense of humor). Instead, we select messages that are appropriate for the individual(s).

Before we go into a meeting with a list of prepared names, an important question you need to ask is "What does the 'next step' look like?" In other words when you look at each individual's name on your list, you need to give careful thought to what each person on that list needs. What is each one's "next step?"

The next step for some is to invite them back the next week for worship. The next step for someone else might be to invite him to come on a Wednesday night. The other person on your list already comes to church on Sundays and Wednesdays. What he needs is for someone to wait for him at the door, talk to him, and sit with him when class or worship begins.

The next step for others might be an invitation to do something outside of a church building (after all, that's when relationships are built). They may need you to invite them to go see that movie that a handful of people from church are going to see on Saturday night, or to go grab ice cream after church on Wednesday night. The next step might even be to invite them over to your house to eat (see Zacchaeus in Luke 19 or Tanner in Chapter 10 of this book!).

Someone from your congregation went forward last week asking for prayers. The next step had better be for someone (an elder, minister, anybody!) to follow up with him, letting him know that you care, and that you're praying for him.

Another person from your congregation lost a loved one yesterday. What's the next step need to be? Can you go to the funeral, send a card, or take them a meal?

Some others haven't been to church in six months. It might be difficult to know what the next step needs to be, but do something! They need to know that they are important and that you care.

Someone else came to church for the first time three months ago and he has come every Sunday and Wednesday since. What's the next step? Perhaps it's time to see if he would like to sit down and study about becoming a Christian.

Other next steps might include: a phone call or a text asking how someone is doing (some people are waiting for you to ask, and to really mean it), encouraging someone after the loss of a job, offering someone a more reliable mode of transportation to church (like offering him a ride), a text thanking a guest for coming for the first time, or an encouraging Bible verse to a new Christian.

There have even been times where the next step has been to "cool it." If you don't get a response after sending your 15th text in a row, there's probably a reason! Don't harass them. There is such a thing as being annoying and pushy, and also know that some people aren't interested in being reached.

If we want to move people closer to the Lord, we don't need to push them away, and sometimes the best thing to do is to be patient and let it lie.

. . . .

HOW YOU SAY IT

The other aspect of the follow up process that we give attention to is how that "next step" is communicated.

It's amazing how many so Christians with good intentions can cause so much damage.

How many times have you been "cornered" by someone and been asked, "Hey! Where were you last week?"

"Where have you been?"

"Man, when was the last time **you** were here?"

"Class (or retreat or lock-in) was so great last week! Why don't you ever come anymore?"

While many of those statements look a little harmless, there's a hint of guilt in each of them. Instead of making people feel guilty for missing (many of those who need encouragement already feel terrible about themselves and/or about missing), we encourage the Lunch Ladies to encourage them...almost to a fault!

Every May we take our juniors and seniors on a retreat to Gatlinburg and talk to them about their legacy and about their faithfulness in the college years and beyond. On the year that Lunch Ladies launched, we only had three Lunch Ladies on that trip.

On Saturday evening, we turned off the lights, had a devotional, and at the end of the night, let the juniors and seniors share whatever was on their hearts. After a few minutes, one particular senior girl, one who wasn't very faithful in attending church, spoke up, and what she had to say caught my ear.

"I just wanted to say--" she began, as she choked back tears "--that I have missed so much church...like a lot...and...I need to do better about coming...I've...just...had a really hard time lately dealing with some things...and I know that that's an excuse. I really regret not coming more...but...every week I get the nicest text from Emilie and Claire telling me how much they miss me and just asking how I'm doing...not to make me feel guilty...but just to see how I am...and...it...just means the world to me."

I couldn't help but smile. How cool that this senior girl would mention how much that impacted her (unsolicited), and the two girls she mentioned weren't even there to hear it.

LUNCH LADIES MEETING EXPECTATION #6
PRAY.

Like we mentioned back in Chapter 13, if prayer, the means by which we inquire of God's power, is not a part of this process, we will fail (Psalm 127:1).

You must pray. Ask God for things; ask Him for more than you can think (Ephesians 3:20), and take note of the ways that He is at work---that's where you'll begin in your meeting next week (celebration). It's beautiful and fitting that the fourth major part of the meeting is prayer--every meeting begins with celebration (thanksgiving to God), and ends in supplication (petitioning of God).

LUNCH LADIES MEETING EXPECTATION #7
CHEER.

Okay, this one's negotiable, but the cheer I ripped from DeVries' book works well for teenagers! "1, 2, 3! We feel awkward so you don't have to!"

LUNCH LADIES MEETING EXPECTATION #8
END EARLY.

Early on in this ministry I made the mistake of doing Lunch Ladies meetings from 6:30-7:00, all the while encouraging them to work the room and greet people and make sure nobody got left out.

How much sense does it make to tell people that and not give them time to do it?!? Zero sense. It took me about a year and half to realize how foolish that was.

Now our meetings end 15 minutes before class starts (we meet from 6:15-6:45), so that they can do the very thing that we are meeting about: minister to people (meet new people, reach out to loners, the shy, etc.).

LUNCH LADIES MEETING EXPECTATION #9
ENJOY IT!

A part of me wonders if this even needs to be a meeting expectation, but I think it has to be!

Good luck leading this ministry if you don't have fun with it. Yes, looking after souls is serious business, but if the sights and the stories of other people that are striving to fulfill God's will by ministering to souls don't put you in a good mood, I'm not sure what will!

I have to share an idea here that you might try out or improve upon that has been so much fun for our team.

As I mentioned before, every fall we bring in new recruits. But there have been several times where we have brought in some new Lunch Ladies during the middle of the school year. These recruits are people in which we have seen tremendous growth over the course of time and have proven themselves ready to become part of the ministry. We figure, "Why wait an entire year if someone is ready to be an asset to this ministry immediately?"

And so we have a little fun with them. I call the new recruit(s) and tell them I need them to come to a meeting where I want to talk to them about something important about the youth group. That's all. I also ask them not to say anything to anybody about it.

Once the time of the meeting rolls around, they walk into a meeting that they know nothing about, while the rest of us know everything. I explain the real reason behind the meeting, tell a short version of how the Lunch Ladies came to be, and then we give them a big spatula (or some kind of "Lunch Lady-esque" kitchen utensil) and pass it around the room from person to person. Each person talks about why they think that the new recruit(s) will be an asset to our mission.

One night, one of our excited new recruits went back and shared with her mom, "Mom, I used to be on the list--now I have a list!"

Loosen up. Stay positive. Laugh. And enjoy the ride.

17

FAILURE TO LUNCH
(WHAT TO DO WHEN SOMETHING'S NOT WORKING.)

THE SORCERER'S APPRENTICE

The most famous scene from Walt Disney's *Fantasia* (and one of the most famous scenes in Disney history) is called "The Sorcerer's Apprentice" (if you've seen it, the music is probably ringing in your ears right now!). You've probably seen it, or least seen the trademark pointy, blue hat with stars and moons atop Mickey Mouse's head.

The cartoon begins with a powerful sorcerer leaning over a cauldron, waving his hands and calling forth great magic. Then the camera pans to the sorcerer's apprentice Mickey Mouse, who is handling sorcerer's apprentice responsibilities, and while I'm not entirely sure what all his job description entails, in this particular scene he is struggling to carry two buckets full of water through the dark, narrow corridors of his workplace.

With every step he takes, water sloshes about, and after some time, an exhausted Mickey sets the buckets down, wipes the sweat from his brow, and looks over to admire the sorcerer's handiwork. Smoke from the cauldron rises into the air, and with the wave his hand, the sorcerer beckons forth a large, winged creature. The wizard lifts his hands higher into the air and as the smoke continues to rise, the creature takes shape, becoming a large, colorful butterfly.

And then with the flick of his wrist, the entire butterfly unfolds into a million colorful pieces, each of them landing back in the pot. The pot is calm now, and the sorcerer takes a break, leaving behind his glowing blue magical cap next to the cauldron.

Mickey can't help himself. He tiptoes over to make sure that his master is away, and hurries excitedly towards the hat. Without hesitation he puts it on and does his best sorcerer impression, eyeing first a nearby broom in a corner. He stares it down with a determined look, lifts his hands into the air, and tries to muster all of the magic he can. Suddenly, the broom is "awakened," and before long the sorcerer's apprentice has an apprentice of his own: a magical broom trained to carry heavy buckets full of water and to dump the water into a large cauldron.

Mickey dances about the room elated. He is proud of himself, and his plan is working smoothly, so smoothly in fact, that he decides to kick back in a chair and relax. And why shouldn't he? After all, he has been working hard, and now everything was working perfectly. The sorcerer's apprentice falls asleep and dreams of bigger and better ways to use his newfound magic.

When he finally wakes up, it's too late. The broom has continued to do what it was "supposed" to be doing, but now the floor is completely covered with water and everything is a mess. Mickey starts to panic. He runs over to the broom and tries casting another spell on it, but he's unsuccessful and the broom doesn't respond. Now, Mickey knows he needs to do something drastic and do it fast before this thing gets completely out of hand, so in desperation he takes an axe and chops the broom to smithereens.

Whew. Close one.

But to his horror, the broom multiplies, and now dozens of unstoppable brooms are marching forward with pails in hand, continuing to add to the heap of water now flooding the quarters.

I'm afraid "The Sorcerer's Apprentice" is an all-too-familiar parable in ministry.

. . . .

REALITY CHECKS

You excitedly "run towards the wizard's cap" because (fill in the blank) is happening. Maybe what goes in the blank is a new ministry, mission work, or outreach opportunity; maybe it's new staff, or deacon(s), or elder(s), or maybe it's growth.

But then (fill in the blank) happens. Maybe the new ministry isn't led correctly, the mission work is dropped, or the outreach opportunity is poorly supported. Maybe the new staff member(s) didn't stay, or the deacon wasn't quite the leader that you thought he would be, or the elder resigned because he "couldn't take it anymore." Maybe the growth plateaued, and then a steady downward trend began. Maybe you trained a broom to fetch a pail of water, but the room became so full that you started to drown.

What happened?!?

As you might have learned by now, it doesn't take long for issues to arise in ministry. Ministry is messy because it involves people, and people are messy because they have feelings. In ministry, you must also constantly monitor things to make sure they are running smoothly (ask your elders!).

If you are running excitedly towards the wizard's cap, ready to see what the Lord can do (He can do more than you think) after you get this Lunch Ladies ministry off the ground, don't be surprised when you run into issues. Every ministry has issues, because we (people again!) have issues!

I have a feeling that if the sorcerer had it to do over again, he would've talked to Mickey a little bit more about the hat he was so excited about trying out. In this chapter I want to be sure to tell you a little bit more about the hat you're getting ready to try on, so that you won't get overwhelmed and drown, so that you'll know what to expect, and so that you'll be ready to roll with the punches when something doesn't go like you planned.

. . . .

1. BE CAREFUL.

One of the most beautiful, unique, and rewarding things about ministry is that it is all about working with people. It is also the most difficult, frustrating, and unpredictable thing. And all of that goes back to that word that we mentioned a moment ago: *feelings*.

When you're reaching out to people, be careful with your words. In Lunch Ladies meetings, avoid gossip (remember the covenant?) and when encouraging people, avoid guilt trips, canned compassion, and condescending tones. Check yourself, and remember, "Encourage to a fault."

2. BE RELENTLESS.

Before you pick up the cap, remember: God's work is hard work.

At times, convincing people to do God's will is hard (see the prophets of the Old Testament). If Jesus had a tough time with it, chances are you will, too. The good news is Jesus never said it would be easy. In fact, if there was one thing He was always clear about in His ministry, it was this: If you wanted to follow Him, it was going to be hard (cf. Matthew 7:13-14; Luke 8:57-62; Matthew 10:32-39; etc.).

Yes, God's work is hard. It is heartbreaking. It is time-consuming. It is inconvenient. It will cost you. It is messy. It is frustrating. It is tiring. It is stressful.

And yes, Satan is relentless.

So you must be--for a soul is worth everything.

3. DON'T SLEEP ON THE JOB.

It's going to be tempting for you to kick back and relax once this ministry gets going, but remember what happened when Mickey did?

You can be an All-Pro wide receiver, but every single time you take your eyes off the ball, you're going to drop it. The moment that you take your eyes off this ministry, you're going to drop a ball. You might get by for a period of time while the brooms continue to work, but it won't take long for everything to be in disarray.

You can take this to the bank: It doesn't matter what ministry it is, it will not thrive without a strong, capable leader.

When ministries struggle for a period of time, there is usually a wakeup call not far behind...and if there isn't, be prepared to drown! Hopefully we get our wake up call before it's too late and the ministry becomes "that thing that we used to do that was a good idea."

4. DON'T TAKE AN AXE TO YOUR WORKERS.

Mickey in his frustration ended up "killing the work" he started by attacking the one who was there to help serve.

There are going to be times where you are going to see some old habits creep back into the group. It's natural for us to form friendships with a circle of friends. Remember that Jesus had a group within the group of Apostles that he seemed to spend a little more time with in Peter, James, and John.

The problem arises, however, when neglect begins to take place (Esmin Green).

Watch out for this at all times. I don't think I have to remind you of how toxic that kind of behavior can be. It might even be that the Lunch Ladies themselves begin to slip into old habits, only talking to each other, or only talking to a specific person or group of people.

Instead of "taking the axe" to them, share with them your concerns (they've probably noticed the old habits, too) and gently remind them of the reasons why ministry was created in the first place. There may be times when you need to "hold up the covenant" and go back over it (that's what the prophets did, right?).

Instead of bossing them around, work alongside of them.

Instead of preaching at them, pour into them.

Instead of supposing that they know how to minister to people, show them how to minister to people.

Also bear in mind that the Lunch Ladies are just like everybody else: they struggle. In your pursuit of souls, don't neglect the ones inside the room (and don't neglect your own soul either). There have been times when some of our Lunch Ladies have needed to step aside from being a Lunch Lady for a while. I always assure them that this is okay, and tell them to take all of the time that they need. I also make sure to tell them that as soon they are ready to jump back in, the invitation is on the table, because we need them.

One more quick note here: I never, ever, ever make someone feel guilty/bad about missing a meeting. Sometimes life happens. Sometimes they have a game. Sometimes they have to work. Sometimes they get sick. Sometimes they get stuck in traffic, or their car gets messed up. Sometimes, they go and do something terrible like pick up a friend for worship!

Remember, the Lunch Ladies are on your team. So put away your axe: don't take your frustrations (and maybe even your own shortcomings) out on them.

5. DON'T BE AFRAID TO ASK FOR HELP.

The reason I aspired to write this book in the first place is because I want to see God's church reach people, and I have seen the way that God has used this ministry to reach people.

If I have made the implication that implementing, leading, and continuing the Lunch Ladies ministry is a piece of cake, then I haven't been real with you. It's challenging work, work that makes you feel like you're riding on a carousel of emotions--overjoyed, overwhelmed, frustrated, hopeful, and exhausted to the point that you're ready to take a good, long nap. Come to think of it, it makes you feel like the sorcerer's apprentice.

I'm not an expert when it comes to this ministry, and it has been my prayer from the very beginning of this book to not come across like I am. However, I am sort of an expert when it comes to making mistakes. I hope that you have been able to learn from some of my hits and misses.

If I can be of assistance to you in any way, in beginning or in troubleshooting this kind of ministry, I'd love to have the opportunity to help. My email address is philmycup@hotmail.com. As you might've guessed, this is my favorite subject to talk about, so feel free to email me anytime.

Also, we have lunched (see what I did there?) a Lunch Ladies Facebook page where we are asking you guys to join us in celebrating God's successipes! Think of it as a way for all of us to sit in on Lunch Ladies meetings happening all across the nation and celebrate together! I'd love to hear how God is using a ministry like this to reach people where you are.

So what are you waiting for? We've got lots to celebrate! Visit "Lunch Ladies Ministries" on Facebook, and post away!

6. DON'T QUIT!

Chances are you've taken some sort of medication before that your body didn't respond to in the right way.

What did you do when that happened? Did you quit the medicine? "That's it! What a waste of my time! Medicine just doesn't work and I have had it! I'm through with this! I'm never taking any medicine ever again!" Nobody says that, well, at least nobody that I've ever met.

In the medical field, doctors, surgeons, and health-care professionals understand that sometimes they have to change their approach. Maybe a patient had an allergic reaction to the first medication that he was prescribed. Maybe the dosage wasn't right. Maybe the patient experienced some side effects.

In these cases, it wasn't necessarily the medicine's fault, the patient's fault, or anybody else's fault: the body just didn't respond to it in the right way.

In ministry, some things will be your fault, and some things won't. Whatever category the shortcoming falls under, remember: don't quit the medicine. You wouldn't sell your car if it ran out of gas. By the same token, don't make the decision to nix a soul-searching ministry like Lunch Ladies just because something needed to be adjusted. The truth is even the greatest ideas need to be tweaked, reworked, and improved upon--imagine if nobody had tweaked, reworked, or improved the telephone, the automobile, or the airplane!

Whatever you do, don't quit the medicine: the ministry!

And don't quit on people either!

Perhaps this is the unspoken message that has run throughout the course of the book. It is in every story. It is on every page.

I mentioned that Chris and I spent months studying together before he became a Christian. There were times where I thought he would **never** obey the Gospel (in fact, I can recall one retreat where he basically said that in front of the entire group).

Keep praying. Keep loving. Keep investing.

And don't quit on new Christians either!

Babies need a lot of checkups. Pediatricians recommend that newborns visit the doctor for a 1, 2, 4, 6, 9, and 12-month checkup. Nobody in a new baby's family would hug the child and say, "Welcome to our family! Now, good luck!" and never to speak to them again. Babies don't come out of the womb knowing how to feed themselves, how to talk, how to walk, or how to care for themselves.

That's where we come in! God knew we would need a team, the church, a community of saved people to help us learn how to grow.

I cherish and love the stories of baptism in this book, but our stories are not meant to end in baptism. In fact, the Bible calls us "new creations." The stories shared in this book are not fairy tales where "they all lived happily ever after." Everybody's story has messy parts, and new Christians are going to have their struggles. That doesn't mean that they've ruined the beautiful story God is telling.

Don't quit on them.

Keep praying. Keep loving. Keep investing.

Nobody's story is finished until the Author of Life says so.

18

THE BOOK IS ENDING.
THE STORY IS NOT.

WONDER FULL TONIGHT

I'm trying hard tonight to get into a reflective mood. Eighteen chapters into the book, I guess it just feels like what I should be doing. But for some reason I'm not in reflective mode. I'm in question mode. I'm wondering things like:

Who are you? Where are you from?

Why are you reading this book? Has it helped you? Has it challenged you? Have you enjoyed it? Has it been a waste of time?

What is going through your mind after seventeen chapters? What questions do you have?

Do you want to start a Lunch Ladies ministry? If not, why not?

Are you a minister? If so, what challenges are you facing in your ministry and how does this book fit into the equation? Are you a seasoned veteran looking for fresh ideas, or are you a rookie just starting out in ministry (and if so I sort of envy you! I wish I had known about the Lunch Ladies when I first started!)?

And then there's this question: With whom do you need to share this book?

Chances are you know someone that has the heart of a Lunch Lady, a heart that beats for souls in big, beautiful ways. Perhaps it's been hard not to think about that person as you've read. Perhaps you've already been telling them about this book. It fires me up to think about what those kinds of people with those kinds of hearts will do with this kind of book! I've mentioned it many times, but there's truly no limit to what God can do with a willing heart.

I've spent a lot of time dreaming about the different groups of people that might get their hands--no, **their hearts**--on this book! Imagine the possibilities!

What if ministers get their hands on this book?

Maybe it's a no brainer, but a youth minister may be the most natural person to consider giving a copy of this book. Maybe he is or has been in a similar situation to where I was when I began this story: feeling like the teacher of a random collection of students inside of a high school cafeteria. Sure, there's a chance this book will sit on his desk for a few weeks (ahem, cough), but maybe, just maybe, this one will be a blessing to his youth ministry.

But you know what? Drop the word *youth* from the above description: this is a book about ministry. It will resonate with ministers.

What if every minister in the church started leading a ministry similar to Lunch Ladies in our congregations?

It wouldn't just change youth groups, it wouldn't just change churches, it wouldn't just change the world--it would change **eternities**.

Why? **Not because of how great this ministry is, but because of how great our God is.** We must remember that it is our Father's business--we just work in it!

What if elderships get their hearts on this book?

I'm no elder, but I've sat inside of enough elders' meetings to know that many of the themes in this book are the stuff of an elder's heart. Elders are in the sheep business. By their very definition they are to be shepherds.

I don't know exactly what it would look like if every man who has been commissioned by God to shepherd His people would get his heart on this book, but I do have some idea of what it looks like: Might I remind you that our eldership believed in this ministry's concept so much that we are now doing it on a congregation-wide level?! I believe it speaks volumes about the men's hearts who shepherd us at Mt. Juliet.

What if youth groups get their hearts on this book?

Well, this one's sort of an easy one to visualize, considering there is an entire book to tell the tale! By the way, isn't it weird how easy it is to forget that this is a story about youth ministry? I constantly have to remind myself that these are high school students I'm talking about here! The hearts of our students continually blow me away.

What if churches get their hearts on this book?

When I first began thinking about this book, I thought it might be challenging to write something that everybody, not just youth ministers, could use. But with every turn of a page I began to realize that this isn't just a book for youth ministers, although I hope every youth minister will read it. Neither is it a book for ministers, although I think every minister ought to read it.

This is a book for Lunch Ladies.

But wait a minute, who are Lunch Ladies?

Lunch Ladies are people with willing hearts that are serious about winning souls.

In case you haven't figured it out yet, I'll let you in on a little secret: Lunch Ladies are Christians!

For this ministry I didn't "invent" a new kind of person--God did! **Christians are saved people who want to save people.** Christians surrender their will for His, and if that means "feeling awkward" for the sake of a soul, so be it! Christians will do whatever it takes to win a soul.

As Paul stated, "I have become all things to all people, that by all means I might save some. I do it all for the sake of the Gospel, that I may share with them in its blessings" (1 Corinthians 9:22b-23).

Yes, this is a book about soul winning, a book for churches, a book for Christians.

. . . .

THE ROLLER COASTER

Perhaps the reason that I'm having such a hard time getting into reflective mode and putting the finishing touches on this book is because it's difficult to find a way to wrap a story that's still being written.

You might've noticed as you read this book how many times words like *last week*, *yesterday*, and *tonight* appeared. It seems like whenever I was ready to wrap up a story, God would begin writing another incredible one, and similarly, just when I knew how a chapter needed to end, God would tack on another incredible twist.

I'm clearly not the One in charge here.

This ministry all comes full circle, back to the roller coaster ride that I mentioned in the preface. Perhaps at this point, you've decided that you'd like to ride the roller coaster as well. That's what I've been praying!

Before your car leaves the station, there are five things I want to say to you, so allow me to get on the microphone and mutter some things through the muffled speaker about how important it is to keep your hands and feet inside the cart at all times and such...

1 **You've got an Esmin Green.**

This has been one of the main points behind the story from the very beginning. Chances are there's someone that you need to see. And the converse of that statement may be even truer: chances are there's someone that needs you to see them.

Who is your Esmin Green and what are you going to do about it?

2 **Pray.**

Is there any way I can overemphasize the role of prayer? Even praying about the same thing over and over is Christlike--in Matthew 26 Jesus prayed three times (that we read about!) for the cup of suffering to pass from Him if it were God's Will.

Starting a Lunch Ladies ministry? Bathe it in prayer. When we pray, "more than we think" happens, and answers come "out of the blue" when we least expect it.

3 **Salvation begins with an invitation.**

"If they can't hear it, it doesn't matter."

Nobody obeys a Gospel that they've never heard (Romans 10:14), and nobody visits a church that they've never heard about either. The only reason you are a Christian is because someone invited you. God sent out the invitations to His feast, but He put them in our hands. It's up to you and me to pass them out. And remember, God's servants are not the ones who get to decide who's on His guest list.

4 **Don't quit.**

Today I had one of those days that made me wish someone else had written this book.

I got a call from an upset parent whose child got her feelings hurt because she was left out of something. I listened, apologized, and assured her that I wanted things to be better, and that we would work harder at making sure that something like this wouldn't happen again.

I felt for the girl. I had seen this one coming, and I had a bad feeling about it in the pit of my stomach all weekend long. But by the time I discovered what was happening, it was too late. The damage had been done. And to make matters worse, it wasn't the first time that this girl had felt neglected.

I hate when stuff like this happens. Absolutely hate it. One reason is I've been there, and I remember what it feels like to be neglected. Another reason I hate it is now we have a ministry designed to help make sure that things like this don't happen anymore.

Just as I was getting ready to put the finishing touches on this book, today came and reminded me of an important, harsh reality: it doesn't matter who you are, or what you do, you cannot reach everybody.

You could give people all of your attention. You could speak to them constantly. You could send them the greatest gift in the world. You could follow up with them regularly. You could dream up an entire ministry for them. You could give them exactly what they ask for.

Still, you cannot reach all.

Want proof? God.

God has given us His undivided attention, spoken to us constantly, sent us the greatest gift in the world, follows up with us regularly, and gives us many of the things that we ask for. He has done all of those things and He has done much, much more, yet still many refuse Him.

Want more proof that it doesn't matter who you are, or what you do, you cannot reach everybody? Jesus.

The world's greatest minister to ever walk on the face of the earth wasn't able to reach everyone, and even if you rose up from the dead, there would still be people that would reject you.

"Okay! So it doesn't matter who I am, or what I do, I can't reach everybody! Jesus couldn't either, so why bother? We might as well quit!"

No. The answer, once again, is to consider what Christ did.

He knew He wouldn't be able to reach everybody, but what did He do? He prayed anyway. He served anyway. He preached anyway. He sacrificed anyway. He loved anyway. He gave of Himself anyway.

He did everything that He could anyway.

Satan tried getting Jesus to quit, and he would love it if you would quit, too.

Don't.

Pray anyway. Serve anyway. Preach anyway. Sacrifice anyway. Love anyway. Give of yourself anyway.

Do everything that you can anyway.

And God will give the increase.

 The book is ending, but the Story isn't...so buckle up!

The task is daunting.

"Go therefore and make disciples of all nations, baptizing them in the name of the Father and of the Son and of the Holy Spirit, teaching them to observe all that I have commanded you" (Matthew 28:19-20).

Go? Go and do what?

Make disciples.

Go and make disciples? Where?

All nations.

It was daunting then. It is daunting now.

"The harvest is plentiful but the workers are few," Jesus said.

Sometimes it feels as if we are tremendously outnumbered and understaffed.

Well, we are and we aren't.

We are outnumbered. But so was Noah, so was Elisha (or so it seemed! [2 Kings 6:8-23]), so were the Israelites (in seemingly every story!), so were Shadrach, Meshach, and Abednego, and so were the Twelve.

We're outnumbered. Big deal. I like our chances.

But we are not understaffed. No, not by a long shot. For when we have the courage for faithful obedience, for doing God's will, God blesses us. When we follow Him, He takes care of us (He's the Good Shepherd), and He allows us to be a part of some incredible stories for His glory.

A boat ride that saved the world. An army with chariots of fire. Watery walls that provided safe passage in a story that would have otherwise had a dead end (literally). Fireproof faith. A lifesaving Gospel to spread.

What if the only thing that's missing from someone's story is you? The way most people are going to meet Christ is by meeting a Christian. The Alexes of the world need the Graces of the world.

Some have already heard about Jesus. What they need is for you to show them who He really is. **There is no substitute for the simple,**

iconic, unmistakable, authentic love of Christ. It is not called "the love of Christians." It's called "the love of Christ."

Christians, we've got work to do.

The book is ending. But the Story is not.

Tell it.

And write it upon the hearts of those you meet.

To God be the story.

APPENDIX I:
F.A.Q.S

> *"Can a Lunch Ladies ministry operate on a congregation-wide level? How does that work?"*

Yes. At Mt. Juliet, we have a ministry fashioned after the Lunch Ladies called "All For One." Here's a little bit about it:

The Name: The ministry is called "All for One" because to the shepherd, the chance to save one sheep was enough to leave behind 99 others; to the woman, finding one lost coin was worth pulling an all-nighter with a lamp and a broom in hand tearing an entire house apart; and to the Father, the one rebellious son's return was worth a ring, a robe, a feast, and a celebration.

The Good Shepherd, the diligent woman, and the loving Father did it all for one, and if we want to be compassionate, courageous, and caring like the Good Shepherd, if we want to be diligent, relentless workers like the woman, if we want to be welcoming, forgiving, and loving like our heavenly Father, we, too, must be "all for one."

The Structure: Every Sunday morning adult Bible class has an All For One ministry. The All For One groups meet every two weeks and get together to celebrate, update, invest, and pray. They zero in on reaching people that are natural fits for their demographic. For example, if a young married couple moved into the area and visited Mt. Juliet, it would be natural for our Sunday morning Bible class loaded with young married couples to be the class to follow up and reach out to them.

Also of note, due to our congregation's shepherding model, every adult Bible class has an elder in it, who is closely connected to the members inside of that room. It sounds like a small detail, but has paid off big dividends having our shepherds more closely connected to the flock; it has helped our membership and eldership build a relationship.

Finally, every adult Bible class also has a class coordinator. One of the roles of the class coordinator is to be in charge of "running the meeting." So it is important for this person to have a good grasp of what the purpose of the All For One ministry is.

> "How do you find people for this ministry especially in the beginning when the culture is so exclusive/divided? It seems hopeless at first to find a group of kids that will reach out/ put themselves out that much to do this."

Until people are sick of the circumstances (of neglect, exclusivity, and division), why would they change? I promise I'm not trying to make light of any situation, but you might compare the rehabilitation process of your youth program to the rehabilitation process of an addict. An addict will not go to rehab and make changes until they are ready. Sadly, it doesn't really matter how much **you** want things to be better. It's on them. And if we do not realize the toxicity of "a culture of indifference," we can come to expect more Esmin Green-like stories.

I know it can feel hopeless to find a group of people (kids) that will reach out and put themselves out there. But remember, Jesus used 12 willing men to change, not just a culture, but a **world**! Do what Jesus did: look for those that are looking for something better. God will work through their willing hearts, and if God gives you one willing heart, it's always better than 100 unwilling hearts. There are a lot of Bible stories where God used one willing heart to reach thousands of other hearts.

Remember to be patient and encourage your fellow culture-vators of the Actsmosphere! Growing a seed (an individual) takes time. Growing an entire forest (a culture) takes a long time. God will work with what you have, and He'll give you what you need to carry out His will.

> "I've got 4 kids in my youth group. What would this ministry look like for a small group?"

I think it would be an intimate adventure! Allowing your students to dream a little bit about the way that things could be is exciting! I think you could have meetings with that group every week and every week keep on praying, celebrating progress, making investments, and giving updates on how things are going.

> "Can't middle school kids do this, too?"

When I first started this ministry I constantly considered this concept, because as so many have learned already, there is plenty of work to do, and not a lot of workers!

Having said that, I am so thankful we never started a Lunch Ladies for middle school students.

Personally, I don't recommend launching a Lunch Ladies ministry for your middle school students. I love middle school students, but as a general rule, they aren't capable of much tact, and tact is attribute to possess when it comes to this ministry. It's important for them to know how to handle themselves, handle the information that might come up in a meeting.

"Hey, guess what?!? We were talking about you last night at church and I want you to know that we are praying for you to be more faithful to God since you don't come here very much!"

Like I said--- "tact."

I know that freshmen in high school haven't mastered that word, but they seem to be closer to understanding the concept than a middle school student.

A better alternative to accomplishing things on a middle school level, I've learned, has been to call one or two of them up on the phone and ask them for their help on a "secret mission" to reach out to so-and-so. Seems to work very well with that group.

> **"My high school and middle school kids are combined. Can I do this with a mixed- aged group?"**

I think I would start with the high school students first and see how that goes. You cannot "uninvite" people from being part of this ministry but you can always open up the invitation later.

> **"How do you keep up with the people you are trying to reach out to?"**

Bear with me, because this is an important one!

First I have a master youth ministry directory (it's actually a Google spreadsheet online that allows our staff the ability to make corrections or additions to it) that consists of everybody that ever comes to anything ever. We have little guest cards that we give out on Sundays and Wednesdays and ask our guests to turn them in. In fact, if they turn it in, we give them a t-shirt just as a little way of saying "Thanks for coming!"

Our master directory has around 400 names in it. What this does is create a huge database of information to pull from.

This is your step one. You need to be able to pull a list out that has **everybody** represented in it, whether it's on a congregational level (or Sunday school class) or a youth group level.

The next thing we do is go over every name in the directory and put names into one of four categories. Every cell is in one of four colors.

> White: If your name is in white, it means we don't ever see you.
> Yellow: If your name is in yellow, it means that we sometimes see you.
> Green: If your name is in green, it means that we usually see you.

Blue: If your name is in blue, it means that we are just starting to see you (think new guests).

This data will help you build roll sheets so that you can watch people's attendance trends.

I look at our Master Directory about every two weeks, keeping a close eye on the colors represented. You want names to appear in green, because that color represents a lot of opportunities for spiritual growth. Sometimes names will go from green to yellow (that's not what you want), while other times they will go from blue/yellow to green (that's what you want).

Keeping my eyes on the directory has helped us know which students to watch out for (yellow means "caution"), which ones are starting to get involved (blue), and which ones haven't come to church here in 5 years (white)! It has become a valuable resource for preparing for Lunch Ladies meetings.

"It seems like there are a lot more people in need of an investment, than we have people to invest. How do you prioritize whom you invest in?"

You're exactly right, or more accurately, Christ was right: "The harvest is plentiful but the laborers are few." There is a massive need for ministry and it's just not feasible to get to every name on your master directory every week.

Your "Lunch Ladies list" will have the usual suspects, so you'll need to keep an eye on that master directory so that you can make sure that you're not overlooking the same people every week. That's why directories exist: to show you the people that you are forgetting! Be sure to bring those names up.

As far as prioritizing who to invest in, some investments will be more urgent than others. If someone loses a family member, bump that name up to urgent. It's important to minister to that people during their times of loss. If someone is baptized or asks for prayers, that's an urgent follow up. If someone is a guest, it's urgent for us to follow up the next week.

> "We've had some that I think have the potential to reach out, but just don't. I've often thought inviting them into the Lunch Ladies, what should I do?"

So long as they're a Christian, I'd say invite them and see what happens. Let them see what the meetings are about and how important that they are. They will probably decide whether or not it's for them without getting a "ruling" from you.

You'll also have many that you will want to "will" into becoming Lunch Ladies, but for whatever reason, they will decide not to--some that would have been really great at it! My opinion: don't bother twisting someone's arm about getting involved if they don't buy in.

> "There's this kid in my youth group who is awesome at reaching out to people, but the only thing is, he/she is not a Christian. Think I can still invite him or her into the group?"

Imagine coming back from Disney World pumped up and talking to one of your friends about it and asking: "Hey, have you ever been to Disney World?"

And your friend says, "Oh, yeah! It's awesome! I mean, it's the most amazing place on earth! I love Disney World! It changed my life! I mean, the monorail, the buses, the main gate to the Magic Kingdom–"

And you sort of stop and say, "Wait, what?"

"Oh, yeah! Disney World!"

"Ok, but it doesn't sound like you ever actually entered into Disney World."

"Well, technically, no. But I gotta tell ya, I loved being around it! It sure looked great from the outside looking in!"

There are many in that category when it comes to their relationship with Christ and His church. They may love the events, and they may love the people, but if they are not in Christ, it's like they are standing outside the gate of Disney World thinking they are experiencing it for all it's worth.

The blessings that are found in Christ---until you experience Him, until you experience those blessings--are beyond compare, and when we truly experience Him for all He's worth, there is nothing like it.

Think about it: How can a student who has never followed Christ, convince others to follow Christ? I don't see any reason you should invite him or her to come to the Lunch Ladies meetings.

"How would you turn people away who wanted to be Lunch Ladies but probably aren't ready?"

I probably wouldn't make that call. I'd put the covenant in their hands, tell them to pray about it, and then let them make that call.

"I tell my youth group (or people in the congregation) to invite their friends all of the time, but I just can't get them to invite people!"

We can invite people until we're blue in the face, but if they hate what they get invited to, forget about evangelism.

Perhaps it may be time to consider the fact that things may not be as healthy as you'd like for them to be, and more importantly, as healthy as God wants them to be.

The Department of Children's Services has a huge task and plays an important role in the lives of a lot of children that are in need. One of the things that they must do is enter a home and make a determination about whether or not it is a suitable environment for a child to grow, thrive, and be healthy.

Let ask you a sobering question: Would DCS approve of the way your congregation cares for people?

If they came in, did "home visits" and performed an unbiased study, what would they conclude about the family? Is the home warm and inviting or is it rigid and cold and unwelcoming? Would the congregation be "allowed" to foster spiritual orphans? New Christians--babes in Christ? People who don't know how to care for themselves spiritually? If your congregation adopted a spiritual orphan would they be able to "make it" in your congregation (or youth program)?

That answer may cause you to rethink the culture that exists where you are.

"I'm not sure how to put this, but I think that we have some in our group that would be 'cancerous' to a budding Lunch Ladies ministry. Your suggestions?"

I remember when we first started the Lunch Ladies in Mt. Juliet that there were a couple of students that made me feel the same way. I invited them just like I invited everybody else, but they didn't show up.

I think you ought to invite them, but I wouldn't go beyond sending them the generic text message if you think they will do more harm than good.

"Can the students lead this ministry?"

I have to say that I like the idea of it, but in my experience it hasn't worked for students to "run" it. And once you give thought to the way meetings would be run, you'll probably agree. A 16-year old will have trouble commanding authority inside of that room. He'll be laughed at.

You need to be the one driving the vehicle, not the person with a restricted license.

> "Our meetings are sort of growing stale. How can we shake things up?"

Surprisingly enough, we have dealt with this from time to time. Some things we have done that have been very successful.

When an important, upcoming event (a retreat, church camp, mission trip, etc.) is on the horizon, get that master directory out and make sure that every Lunch Lady leaves with three names of people that they will be sure to invite by the end of the week.

Spend the entire time in prayer, celebrating and supplicating.

Cancel meetings in the summertime or if there is something else significant going on (during the holidays or spring break, or a church-wide event).

> "What do I do if someone randomly shows up to a meeting?"

Roll with it. There's no reason to freak out. This has happened lots of times. When someone shows up that you're not expecting, welcome them and briefly explain how this is a group that meets together and prays every week about how to reach out to people in the youth group and how to help people grow. You could even invite them to come back to the meeting the next week!

> "What do you do when someone repeatedly 'forgot' or 'got too busy' to make the investment into an individual that they committed to making?"

I wouldn't let that response happen two weeks in a row without addressing it. The first week I would give the person a "bye," but if it persisted, I would say something at the beginning of the next Lunch Ladies meeting with a pointed message from my heart about following through.

You definitely don't want "not following through" to become the acceptable norm for the group.

If a few continue to be repeat offenders week after week, even after you've addressed it, I would speak my piece to them in private. I would make the meetings as positive as possible, continue to encourage the ones that are doing what they signed up for, and I would ignore the one that's not.

When it's their time to talk, I would say, "Hey, Will, got anything for us this week?" and if they said "No," I would move on immediately, pretty much ignoring them. When they decide to contribute to the thing that they signed up to contribute to, then I would let them say more.

Don't get me wrong. I wouldn't be a jerk towards them; I just wouldn't react. I'd move on immediately and wouldn't allow them to elaborate on their excuses.

"What kinds of activities does your youth group do?"

We have a website that will give you a ton of insight into our youth ministry. I can assure you that everything we do, and every activity, has a purpose. Check it all out at www.mjyg.org!

"Can I pick your brain?"

Sure! I'd **love** to talk to you some more about this or whatever else I can help with. Hit me up at philmycup@hotmail.com.

APPENDIX II:
PREPARING FOR LAUNCH:
A STEP-BY-STEP CHECKLIST

- **Step 1**: Prepare with prayer.

- **Step 2**: Prepare the soil with a message (or messages) like "Esmin Green," allowing the Word of God to speak to the hearts of your group, convicting them of the need for relevant, relentless, soul-seeking ministry.

- **Step 3**: Set up a meeting after the week of your "Esmin Green" message.

- **Step 4**: Prepare a covenant.

- **Step 5**: Advertise the meeting by sending out an invitation to all Christians who might have willing hearts to be involved in this ministry.

- **Step 6**: Call individuals that you believe may play a big role in this ministry and push hard to get them there.

- **Step 7**: Host your first Lunch Ladies meeting! Make it good!

APPENDIX III:
THE LUNCH LADIES COVENANT

Then He said to His disciples, "The harvest is plentiful, but the laborers are few; therefore pray earnestly to the Lord of the harvest to send out laborers into His harvest" (Matthew 9:37-38).

I. 6:15 meetings every Wednesday...**Be there**!

II. No gossip! This is not a time to get out all the things you hate about people or how much this person annoys you. We are here to talk about how to help the hurt.

III. Reach in---hold yourself accountable! You cannot lead someone to something you are not following yourself!

IV. Reach out---no one goes unspoken to! It's our job to not only make people feel welcome but also included. Remember, we're Lunch Ladies: Love all. Serve all.

V. Follow through---the assignments you take and are given are serious. So follow through with them! This isn't about saying how many people you talked to or about checking someone's name off of a list. This is about making relationships for God!

VI. Bring something to the table. Listen, we're all hungry here, and if you don't bring something to the table, we don't eat. It's that simple. So speak up in meetings! If you're not sharing your thoughts then we don't know what's going on in the kingdom. **You** were asked to be in this group for a reason, so speak up.

VII. Either you're in or you're out. Seriously! This is a group that demands you step up and step out of your comfort zone. Get really comfortable with being really uncomfortable. If you can't handle that, then this isn't the group for you.

I will uphold the Lunch Ladies Covenant to the best of my ability.

Signed: _____

BE SURE TO CHECK OUT
TAKE ROUTE

A BIBLE STUDY BY PHILIP JENKINS
contact Philip at philmycup@hotmail.com

DON'T FORGET TO SHARE YOUR SUCCESSIPES ON THE "LUNCH LADIES MINISTRIES" FACEBOOK PAGE!